Home Networking!

I Didn't Know You Could Do That...™

Erik B. Sherman

SYBEX®

San Francisco • Paris • Düsseldorf • Soest • London

Associate Publisher: Guy Hart-Davis

Contracts and Licensing Manager: Kristine O'Callaghan

Acquisitions & Developmental Editor: Linda Lee

Editor: Diane Lowery

Technical Editor: Donald Fuller

Book Designers: Franz Baumhackl, Kate Kaminski

Graphic Illustrator: Tony Jonick

Electronic Publishing Specialist: Bill Gibson

Project Team Leader: Jennifer Durning

Proofreaders: Kathy Drasky, Dave Nash, Nancy Riddiough

Indexer: Ted Laux

Companion CD: Ginger Warner

Cover Designer: Daniel Ziegler

Cover and Chapter Photographs: PhotoDisc

Library of Congress Card Number: 99-66405
ISBN: 0-7821-2631-6

Manufactured in the United States of America

10 9 8 7 6 5 4 3

Software License Agreement: Terms and Conditions

The media and/or any online materials accompanying this book that are available now or in the future contain programs and/or text files (the "Software") to be used in connection with the book. SYBEX hereby grants to you a license to use the Software, subject to the terms that follow. Your purchase, acceptance, or use of the Software will constitute your acceptance of such terms.

The Software compilation is the property of SYBEX unless otherwise indicated and is protected by copyright to SYBEX or other copyright owner(s) as indicated in the media files (the "Owner(s)"). You are hereby granted a single-user license to use the Software for your personal, noncommercial use only. You may not reproduce, sell, distribute, publish, circulate, or commercially exploit the Software, or any portion thereof, without the written consent of SYBEX and the specific copyright owner(s) of any component software included on this media.

In the event that the Software or components include specific license requirements or end-user agreements, statements of condition, disclaimers, limitations or warranties ("End-User License"), those End-User Licenses supersede the terms and conditions herein as to that particular Software component. Your purchase, acceptance, or use of the Software will constitute your acceptance of such End-User Licenses.

By purchase, use or acceptance of the Software you further agree to comply with all export laws and regulations of the United States as such laws and regulations may exist from time to time.

Software Support

Components of the supplemental Software and any offers associated with them may be supported by the specific Owner(s) of that material but they are not supported by SYBEX. Information regarding any available support may be obtained from the Owner(s) using the information provided in the appropriate read.me files or listed elsewhere on the media.

Should the manufacturer(s) or other Owner(s) cease to offer support or decline to honor any offer, SYBEX bears no responsibility. This notice concerning support for the Software is provided for your information only. SYBEX is not the agent or principal of the Owner(s), and SYBEX is in no way responsible for providing any support for the Software, nor is it liable or responsible for any support provided, or not provided, by the Owner(s).

Warranty

SYBEX warrants the enclosed media to be free of physical defects for a period of ninety (90) days after purchase. The Software is not available from SYBEX in any other form or media than that enclosed herein or posted to *www.sybex.com*. If you discover a defect in the media during this warranty period, you may obtain a replacement of identical format at no charge by sending the defective media, postage prepaid, with proof of purchase to:

SYBEX Inc.
Customer Service Department
1151 Marina Village Parkway
Alameda, CA 94501
(510) 523-8233
Fax: (510) 523-2373
e-mail: info@sybex.com
WEB: HTTP://WWW.SYBEX.COM

After the 90-day period, you can obtain replacement media of identical format by sending us the defective disk, proof of purchase, and a check or money order for $10, payable to SYBEX.

Disclaimer

SYBEX makes no warranty or representation, either expressed or implied, with respect to the Software or its contents, quality, performance, merchantability, or fitness for a particular purpose. In no event will SYBEX, its distributors, or dealers be liable to you or any other party for direct, indirect, special, incidental, consequential, or other damages arising out of the use of or inability to use the Software or its contents even if advised of the possibility of such damage. In the event that the Software includes an online update feature, SYBEX further disclaims any obligation to provide this feature for any specific duration other than the initial posting.

The exclusion of implied warranties is not permitted by some states. Therefore, the above exclusion may not apply to you. This warranty provides you with specific legal rights; there may be other rights that you may have that vary from state to state. The pricing of the book with the Software by SYBEX reflects the allocation of risk and limitations on liability contained in this agreement of Terms and Conditions.

Shareware Distribution

This Software may contain various programs that are distributed as shareware. Copyright laws apply to both shareware and ordinary commercial software, and the copyright Owner(s) retains all rights. If you try a shareware program and continue using it, you are expected to register it. Individual programs differ on details of trial periods, registration, and payment. Please observe the requirements stated in appropriate files.

Copy Protection

The Software in whole or in part may or may not be copy-protected or encrypted. However, in all cases, reselling or redistributing these files without authorization is expressly forbidden except as specifically provided for by the Owner(s) therein.

To Lisa, Allie, and Matthew, who explored the boundaries of patience and tolerance as I wrote this book, and then went a little further.

ACKNOWLEDGMENTS

First and foremost, I want to thank Linda Lee, acquisitions and developmental editor at Sybex, for championing this book and helping to shape it. If she hadn't believed in this project or had given up hope when deadlines looked bleak, these might as well have been blank pages. Guy Hart-Davis, associate publisher, took a chance on a first time book author, and I appreciate it.

Thanks also to the following people:

- Diane Lowery for editing a manuscript prepared in haste and keeping its author from repenting in leisure.

- Donald Fuller for focusing his considerable technical acumen on catching inaccuracies before they could reach the printed page.

- Jennifer Durning for leading the project team.

- Bill Gibson for turning a parcel of files into a book.

- Skye McKay for helping some hare-brained coupon schemes come to fruition.

- Ginger Warner for creating the CD.

- Heather O'Connor for getting some of the CD contents together.

- Kathy Drasky, Dave Nash, and Nancy Riddiough for the thankless and vital task of proofreading.

A number of companies graciously provided products for the CD that made it possible to approach the topic: Alation Systems, Apple Computer, ATI, Benwin, Compaq Computer, Diva, Farallon, General Cable, Hewlett-Packard, Intelogis, MultiTech, NetGear, Security Data Networks, Tecmar, and X10.

Finally, thanks to two people: Marty Winston—technophile masquerading as PR and marketing maven—who brainstormed ideas, whether a client was involved or not, and Richard Small—a fine writer, editor, and friend—whose belief that I would finish on time was positively infectious.

CONTENTS

CONNECT TO YOUR HOME NETWORK ON THE RUN   77

USE YOUR NETWORK TO DELIVER ENTERTAINMENT   103

CONNECT YOUR NETWORK TO THE OUTSIDE WORLD   127

PLAY MULTIPLAYER GAMES ON YOUR NETWORK 275

INTRODUCTION

A caveman once ran over to a neighbor to show his latest invention.

"Look!" said the caveman. "I call it…the *wheel.*"

The neighbor looked the disk over, eyebrows furrowed, and grunted, "So?"

Technology is always ahead of its perceived need. It was years before businesses understood what computer networks could do for them. Today, most companies would be hard-pressed to operate without one.

Now home networks are coming into their own. According to the Yankee Group, a market research firm, soon close to 17 million households could be in the market for one. Home builders more frequently offer to wire new construction for computers, entertainment, and security.

Although this book discusses putting a network into your home, it's really about what you can do with one after it is in place.

What Can Home Networks Do for You?

Networks move information from one place to another. It sounds dull until you realize what that can mean:

- ◆ Everyone can have access to resources such as printers and high-speed Internet connections, which can save you money.
- ◆ You can share schedules, phone books, to-do lists, and other forms of organization.
- ◆ Networks can include far more than a computer, bringing video and audio entertainment to every corner of your home.
- ◆ It's easy to manage recipes and grocery lists on a kitchen server.
- ◆ Multiple people can play computer games against each other.
- ◆ Your business systems can sit in your home.

◆ It's possible to call in from anywhere and have access to your network.

All of these are easy, and this book can show you how to do any of them and more. You'll learn how to set up your network to do almost anything that can come to mind.

Who Is This Book For?

This book is for people who have more than one computer at home, have thought about connecting them together, but then wondered why they should bother. Although readers will learn how to do things, they will, more importantly, see ideas that can spark their own thinking and imagination.

Whatever you may have heard about networks, you don't need to be a dyed-in-the-wool technical savant to make them work. All you need to do is have some patience and the willingness to roll your sleeves up, meta-phorically speaking at least.

What Does This Book Cover?

This book contains 11 parts that cover everything you need to know to use a home network effectively:

Put the Network in Its Place If you don't have a network in place yet, this section shows you how easy it is to install one using cable, your phone lines, wireless connections, or even existing power lines. You can connect Macs to your network or even find uses for older computers.

Get Your Network to Work for You Before getting fancy with your network, see all the use you can get out of it every day. Share files or even applications over your network. Protect your entire network from data loss and viruses. You can keep your hard drives in top shape and make sure you stay legal when using software on your network.

Connect to Your Home Network on the Run Being away from home shouldn't mean that you can't use your network. Whether connecting a hand-held organizer or laptop or dialing in from the road, you can get what you need when you need it. Automation can even keep the most recent copies of files where you need them, when you need them.

Use Your Network to Deliver Entertainment   From MP3 music to putting video on computers, a network can become an extended entertainment center for your home. Store music and video on servers, play Internet radio, automatically enter information about your CDs into a jukebox database, and even create your own CDs.

Connect Your Network to the Outside World   Don't be satisfied with running phone lines to each of your computers. Connect your entire network to the Internet at high speeds. Run an e-mail system or even a Web server directly from your network, and while you do all this, protect kids in your home from the dangers they can face on the Internet.

Use Your Network to Communicate with the World   Communication doesn't end with e-mail and Web surfing. Talk over the Internet, and save long-distance charges, or see the other end of a call with video phones. Manage incoming and outgoing faxes with a fax server, and create a home intercom to someone in another room.

Support Your Home Office with a Home Network   Whether your office is in your home or a building owned by an employer, a home network can help in business. Meet business associates with video teleconferencing, run an e-business off your network, and even provide telephone answering services for yourself. Manage all your business information with state-of-the-art technology, get rid of paper piles, run surveys over the Web or e-mail, and even support a virtual company.

Keep Your Network and Home Secure   You can protect your network and even your home with the technology in this part. Keep communications private from prying eyes, keep a firewall between the network and the Internet, and get central control of all your passwords. You can also plug a home-security system into the network.

Make Your Network an Extended Productivity Tool   A network can make many everyday tasks simpler. Keep common phone books online, add a phone-messaging system so important calls don't go unanswered, and track the household expenses. Plan meals on the network, and automate virtually anything in your home, from lighting to thermostats and appliances.

Set Up a Learning Lab for Children of All Ages   No one is ever too old or young to learn, and a network becomes a tremendous educational tool. Kids can do schoolwork on the Internet or your own network. Screen savers turn down time into learning time. You can turn your network into a virtual planetarium or keep the focus on earth by learning about the weather. Improve your reading, learn music theory, compose your own tunes, and use your own system to enter the high-paying field of networking.

Play Multiplayer Games on Your Network   For many, this might be the first stop. There are many multiplayer games you can host on your network, or you can invite people from the Internet to join in, too. Play card games, strategy games, and arcade favorites.

What You Need for a Network

You will need more than one computer, because a network with one PC is rather limiting, as well as special network-interface cards and perhaps other networking hardware, depending on the type of system you want to install. Though you can use virtually any type of desktop computer on your network, this book assumes that your PCs are running Windows 95, 98, or NT Workstation. After that, it's great if the computers have sound cards, speakers, and even television tuner cards.

Many network applications need special software. Some of this comes with your PC's operating system. Much of the rest can be found on this book's companion CD.

What's on the CD?

 From helpful network utilities and applications to small business software to even games, the CD at the back of this book should keep you busy. Look for the icon next to this paragraph. When you see it, the software discussed in the text at that point is available on the CD. The software is generally for Windows 95, 98, or NT Workstation. If you use another operating system, check the vendor's Web site for availability of other versions.

You can also find special prices and promotions available to you because you own a copy of this book. The coupon pages describe the specials, but to benefit from them, you need the offer redemption information on the CD.

For details on what's on the CD, turn to the last page of the book.

What's on the Companion Web Pages?

The companion page for this book will include all sorts of information, such as interesting network-related products, innovative uses of networks sent in by readers, and the odd bit of news you might find interesting.

To get to the companion page for this book, point your browser to `http://www.sybex.com`. From the home page, click the Catalog button. In the Enter Your Keyword(s) text box, type **2631**, the four-digit International Standard Book Number (ISBN) for this book, and then click the Submit button. Click the listing for this book to get to the companion page.

Terminology and Conventions

To keep this book down to a manageable size, we've used a number of conventions to represent information concisely and accurately:

◆ The menu arrow, ➢, indicates selecting a choice from a menu or submenu. For example, "choose Edit ➢ Preferences" means that you should pull down the Edit menu and select the Preferences item from it.

◆ A + sign indicates key combinations. For example, "press Ctrl+P" means that you should hold down the Ctrl key and press the P key. Similarly, "Ctrl+click" and "Shift+click" indicate that you should hold down the key involved and then click.

- ◆ Typewriter typeface indicates a computer file, directory, Web site, or command.

- ◆ **Boldface** indicates items that you may need to type letter for letter.

- ◆ The words "folder" and "directory" mean the same thing for Windows-based computers.

Home Networks Are Changing

The whole home networking market is booming, and as a result, available technologies and products are changing as fast as weather in New England. This book was published in the fall of 1999, but don't be surprised at changes in what is available for home networks.

The CD has the latest versions of software available when the book was printed, but newer versions may well be available by the time you read this. You can always check the listed Web sites for the latest and greatest.

Have fun, and let us know how your network works out.

Put the Network in Its Place

Few things make it harder to use a home network than not having one. Luckily, networking technology available today makes installing a network an easy hurdle for most consumers. As you will learn in this section, there are many networking choices that will suit homeowners and renters alike and are appropriate for mansions or one-bedroom apartments. There are solutions for those who can host a home remodeling show as well as those who find screwdrivers challenging. You will also find tips on configuring the network after you install it.

1 Become the Network Cable Guy

The typical image of a network is the type found at a business, with cables running through the walls and jacks conveniently placed near power sources. These networks may seem complicated, but they are actually fairly simple. Indeed, they are simple enough to use in your home network.

The basic building blocks of these business-class networks are

Cables The special wires that carry signals from one computer or printer to another.

Network devices Anything attached to the network, including computers, printers, and fax machines.

Network interface cards (NICs) Hardware that allows a network device to send and receive signals over the cables.

Hubs Hardware that connects cables running from network devices and controls the physical communication between them.

Routers Hardware that directs traffic between two networks or, for home users, between the network and the Internet.

Every computer, printer, or fax machine on the network has a NIC either internally installed as a card or externally installed through a connection to either the parallel port or a USB (universal serial bus) interface. Cables run from the NICs to a hub, with the router or perhaps a modem connected to the Internet, as in the figure below.

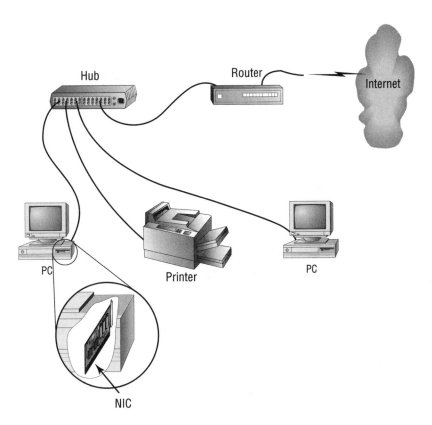

Virtually all cable networks support *Ethernet,* which is an electrical stan-dard for how networks communicate. There are several different network layouts, but the best for a home network is a *star* network. As you see in the illustration above, all network devices connect to a central point, in this case the hub.

When it comes to the networking equipment available to consumers, a star cable network generally uses *10baseT, 100baseT,* or *10/100baseT* products. This means that the network cable, called *unshielded twisted pair,* or UTP, is a special variation on the type of wire telephones use. The cable attaches to the network equipment with *RJ-45 jacks,* which look like a wide version of the plastic jacks that your home phone uses. The initial number refers to the network bandwidth in millions of bits per second (Mbps), so 10baseT carries 10Mbps while 100baseT carries 100Mbps. The last type will work at either 10 or 100Mbps, depending on the speed of the equipment at the other end of the cable.

There are a number of reasons why a star network is the best design for a home network:

◆ UTP is the least expensive type of network cable.

◆ The network equipment and cable have a high capacity to carry data.

◆ It's easy to find compatible equipment in consumer-oriented stores.

◆ UTP is relatively easy to install in most homes.

Cable Network Pros and Cons

Businesses inevitably turn to cable networks for good reasons. Cable offers the highest *bandwidth,* or ability to carry data. Putting this in practical terms, 100Mbps could support a dozen high-speed cable modem connections to the Internet at the same time. Capacity is important when you use audio, video, security, home automation, games, and an Internet connection on a home network at the same time. Using cable provides the greatest flexibility to a network. You can find NICs for virtually any operating system, including DOS, Macintosh, and Linux, as well as Windows 95, 98, and NT.

At the same time, cable can be a pain to install, because you have to pull cables through walls and install jacks. Once in place, cable is not easily moved, so your planning had better be good, with network jacks located where you will need them. You also need to buy equipment that will fit both your needs for today and tomorrow.

Choose the Equipment

You have many choices in cable networks, from the cable itself to network interface cards, hubs, and even kits. Here's a simple rule for choosing network capacity: Don't count the bits, just get the higher capacity. The 100 megabits per second products don't cost much more than the 10 megabits per second varieties, and they provide superior capabilities.

Cable

First pick the cable to use. UTP cable comes in a variety of types—called *categories*—but the most common type for new networks is Category 5, or Cat 5 for short. This type of cable is less expensive and more bendable than most others—a very important feature when you are routing cable through your home. It also works with 100Mbps network equipment. The next drawing shows a 10/100baseT network.

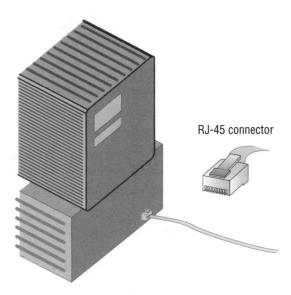

RJ-45 connector

There are other good reasons to use UTP. Because the network is a star, with all devices connecting to hubs, it becomes relatively easy to trace a bad cable because the problem will affect only one device. You can't run UTP cable lengths longer than 100 meters, or a little more than 300 feet, but that shouldn't pose a problem for most homes.

NOTE If you need to run cable further than 300 feet, you can connect two hubs and place them up to 300 feet apart, effectively giving you more distance.

When buying cable, purchase in bulk. You will need lengths not usually found in precut cable, and it will be much cheaper. Be sure that the cable is rated Category 5. This will give you the best shielding from outside electrical interference. If you don't find the price differential too high, consider using Category 5 Enhanced, which has a maximum bandwidth of 1 gigabit per second, or ten times that of plain Category 5. You may not need it now, but if you ever want high-speed networking in the future, it's much easier to replace the network hardware than the cable.

N O T E   In additional to Cat 5, most vendors also carry a *plenum*-rated cable. Far more expensive, this cable has heavy thermal insulation for use inside false ceilings.

N O T E   If you are going to pull cable anyway, consider taking one more step and adding television cable and phone wires. Pulling multiple cables at the same time isn't much more work, and it makes use of any electronics in your house more flexible.

Network Interface Cards (NICs)

Network interface cards are specific in what they support. Most will work with Windows 95/98, and some might support earlier versions of Windows or even DOS.

NICs will be either 8-, or 16-, or 32-bit. The 8-bit cards are an older style and much slower. Don't bother with them; stick to 32-bit, if possible, and get plug-and-play compatible models if using Windows 95 or 98. As much as possible, plan on using the same type card in all your computers. Even plug-and-play might require some adjustments (as specified in the NIC installation instructions). Save yourself the trouble of dealing with two sets of idiosyncrasies.

PCs have different types of *buses,* which are the slots that hold sound cards, video cards, modems, and so on inside a computer. As the drawing below shows, there are two types of buses: ISA and PCI. A NIC will work with one type or the other but not both.

NOTE Newer computers usually have PCI connectors. If your computer has an open PCI connector, get a PCI NIC, because it will run much faster than an ISA NIC.

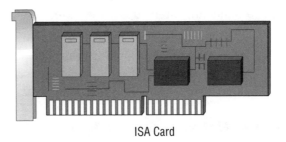

ISA Card

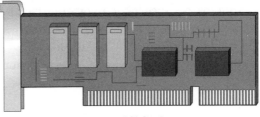

PCI Card

If you don't want to open the computer's case, you can choose devices that plug into a USB port or into the parallel port of a machine. Check specifications to be sure the device will work with your hardware and operating system. There are also PC card NICs that plug into the PC card slots of a laptop, notebook, or handheld. (See the part called "Connect to Your Home Network on the Run" for more information.)

Some printers have a NIC built into them to directly connect to the network, instead of attaching to the parallel port of a computer. If yours doesn't, there is hardware that will connect to the printer's parallel port and then to the network.

Hubs

Also known as concentrators, hubs become the center of your network. All devices on the network will connect to a hub. Besides the choice of 10, 100, or 10/100Mbps bandwidth, you must also choose the number of ports you want. The least expensive hubs have four to five ports, but they are available with a capacity of 16 ports and more. Virtually all hubs can connect to other hubs for expanded capacity. With some designs, you are limited to connecting three hubs. Other hubs with built-in switching technology have no limits on expansion.

When deciding on capacity, leave room for what may come in the future. You can connect hubs together, but it is cheaper to purchase the higher capacity hub in the first place.

Home Network Starter Kits

Some vendors have kits, with "everything" you need. That word is in quotes, because it's actually *almost* everything you need. Although you will get enough NICs and a hub to network some number of computers—typically two computers—the cables won't be long enough to run through the walls. But they will be adequate to either connect the computers within the same room or to the wall jacks you installed.

WARNING Because they usually have only two NICs and a 4- or 5-port hub, kits may be inadequate for your needs. You can solve this by purchasing additional NICs or by buying NICs, a larger capacity hub, and the cables separately.

Design Your Dream Network

Creating a cable-based network takes initial planning. In essence, you want to install a number of RJ-45 jacks, all cabled to a central point where they can connect to the hub. Computers, printers, and other network devices use short cables to plug into jacks and, through them, a hub.

To plan how to run cable, first take a piece of paper and draw a floor plan of your house. Be sure to indicate room dimensions, including height. Mark the locations of electrical outlets, telephone jacks, cable television connectors, and furniture. Choosing the positions for network jacks becomes a matter of trade-offs. You want network jacks located where you might place a computer—by desks, at a telephone, in a convenient spot in your kitchen. Some rooms might be well served with more than one network jack, should you decide to rearrange the furniture.

WARNING Though network devices will almost always be plugged into power outlets, you don't want to locate network jacks next to the plugs, which could cause some interference.

Remember that the total cable length between a network device and a hub—including both the cable between the jack and hub as well as the length of cable between the device and jack—must be under 328 feet (total length). The reason you include room heights in the floor plan is because the cable may have to travel up a wall. Each time a cable runs through a floor into the basement or through a ceiling into an attic in its wanderings, add a couple of extra feet of cable.

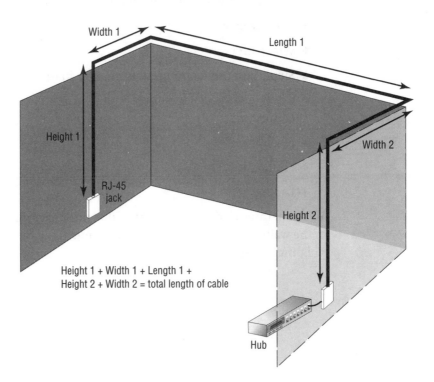

Height 1 + Width 1 + Length 1 + Height 2 + Width 2 = total length of cable

Next, locate your hubs. They should be in an out-of-the-way place, such as a closet or storage area, near a power outlet. If you have an exceptionally large house, or are exceptionally unlucky, you may find some jack or other that would require more than 328 feet of cable to reach the hub. You have three choices:

◆ Add another hub closer to the problem spot and then connect the hubs together.

◆ Reposition a single hub until all jacks are within the proper distance of it.

◆ Reconsider how badly you want a jack in that location.

Install the Cable

Installing cable takes some time, but it doesn't have to be too painful. You will need some tools to get the job done properly. Here is a list that you will find useful:

◆ Hammer

◆ Screw drivers, both Phillips and flat head, of various sizes

◆ Stud finder, which locates the studs by finding the nails in them

◆ Keyhole saw

◆ Wire cutters

◆ Staple gun (for stapling cable in place in the attic or basement)

◆ Crimper, a special tool for stripping insulation from the cable and connecting an RJ-45 connector to a cable end

◆ Electric drill

◆ Flashlight

◆ Ladder

You have three options in running cable through your home: on the inside of the walls, on the outside of the walls, and along the outside of the building.

Good Cabling Practices

Cabling in a devil-may-care fashion will probably put you in hot water sometime in the future, from having loose wires to not knowing where cables lead. A little care at the outset will make life more pleasant.

WARNING Cabling a house may fall under building codes, fire regulations, zoning, or other governmental constraint. Check with officials in your town about legal requirements.

When you run cables along joists or beams in the attic or basement, attach the cables to them. The result is a neat appearance and cables stay out of the way of any additional projects. You can get special hardware for such purposes or even improvise with items like small pipe clamps.

When running a number of cables to a hub, use cable ties where they meet. The ties are plastic strips that can wrap around a number of cables and secure them together. It keeps things neat.

WARNING Label cable ends so you know where they lead. This will save you later aggravation.

Install Cables within the Wall

Installing cable in the walls of your home is definitely the way to go if it is possible. The principle is to open a hole in the wall where you want a jack. You push cable up to the attic or down to the basement, whichever is easier. The cable then runs along and often across the beams called joists, and finally up inside another wall to come out of another jack.

For each jack location, you need an RJ-45 jack, which will probably include a face plate, and a switch box, which sits in the wall and holds the jack and its face plate. Face plates are either metal or plastic; the latter can be fastened within a wall to hold the jack.

You will find a *fish tape* worth the $20 to $30 investment. It is a long, stiff metal line used to pull cable. Unroll a length, put it into a hole in the wall, and then slide it until the end reaches another opening. Clip the cable to the hook on the end, and pull the fish tape back.

NOTE A particuarly good switch box for wiring existing homes is the Carlon model from Lamson & Sessions. Push the box into a properly sized hole in the wall, turn two screws, and plastic tabs bite into the inside of the wall, holding the box in place. For wiring, Ideal makes good crimpers and fish tapes.

You will probably find it easiest to bring the box or roll of cable into the attic or basement and pull the ends down (or up) to the proper locations.

1. Refer to your diagram, and locate the correct spots for the jacks in the actual rooms. Use the stud finder to be sure you have located the jack between studs.

2. Drill a pilot hole, and then use the keyhole saw to cut the right-size opening.

WARNING Work carefully to avoid drilling into power cables, telephone lines, or pipes. If you meet resistance, stop!

3. Unroll 10 or 15 feet of tape, and then push it up to the attic (or down to the basement).

4. Attach a free end of cable to the clip on the end of the fish tape. (This is best done with two people, unless you like running up and down stairs.)

5. Pull on the fish tape and bring the cable into place.

NOTE Be sure to leave a foot or two sticking out from the wall. You can always push extra cable back up into the wall, but there are no cable stretchers to help you if a length is too short.

Follow the instructions included with the RJ-45 jack for connecting the wires in the cable. Because UTP relies on its wires being twisted to cut down outside interference with network traffic, don't untwist any more of an end than you need to connect to the jack—certainly no more than two inches.

Install Cables along the Wall

There are reasons to avoid cutting holes in the wall: not owning the property, avoiding installed pipes and wires, or laziness, to name three.

In such a situation, you can surface mount cable on the wall with special conduit. You cut lengths, fit them together with special connectors and elbows, and mount them to the wall. The cable runs through them. You can use surface mounted boxes (with a jack included) to complete a cable run.

Install Cables outside Your Home

In some older buildings, it may be difficult, if not impossible, to run cable through the walls. You can use surface mounting, but that doesn't help if you need to move from one floor to the next.

In such a case, you can use a cable TV installer's trick and drill though a ceiling (or floor). At times when this is not practical, you might consider drilling a hole in the wall, running a cable along the outside of the building, and pushing it through another drilled hole in another room. It's the least preferable way of cabling, but it may be the only choice in some situations.

NOTE Check with your cable provider for cable that is UL rated for both indoor and outdoor use. General Cable has a special type of Cat 5 UTP called Command Links Plus for indoor or outdoor use.

Add Connectors to a Cable

Eventually you will need cables with RJ-45 connectors on them, either on one end for the cables running to the hub or on both ends to connect a network device to a wall jack. This is where you use the crimper and stripper.

To attach a connector to cable, follow these steps:

1. Cut the cable square at the end and use the stripper to remove the outer insulation. You should now see four multicolored wires: one white with an orange stripe, one orange with a white stripe, one white with a green stripe, and one green with a white stripe.

2. The RJ-45 connector has one end that has room for the cable to enter. The other end has eight pins that fit into the RJ-45 jack. Hold the jack so the pins are facing up and the plastic tab that locks the jack into place faces away from you. The pins are numbered from left to right 1 through 8.

3. Place the white wire with orange stripe into the pin 1 slot. The orange wire with white stripe goes into the pin 2 slot. The pin 3 slot is for the white wire with green stripe. The green wire with white stripe is placed apart from the others in the pin 6 slot.

4. When the wires are in place, put the connector into the crimping tool and squeeze the handle.

Wire the Hub

The other end of each cable running from a jack must attach to a hub. Instead of facing a mass of cables coming out of the wall, consider the professional's approach of a *patch panel*. A patch panel is a box that holds groups of wires that you wish to connect together.

Cables enter one side of the patch panel and connect via *punch down blocks*. Using a special tool, you quickly fasten the cable to the block. Each block is wired to a location on the patch panel. You run cables from the other side to the ports on the hub, adding RJ-45 connectors to the free ends so they can plug into the hub. By using patch cables, you can easily connect different ports to different cables in your house, so if you move a piece of equipment, it's easy to reconnect the equipment to its old port.

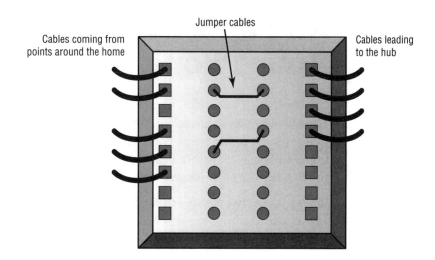

Install a NIC in Each Computer

Although these are general instructions, NICs may have their own peculiarities. Be sure to read the instructions that accompany them. Here is how to install an internal NIC card.

1. Turn off the computer, and unplug the power cord.

2. Open the computer case.

3. Prepare the NIC according to manufacturer's instructions, if necessary, and insert it into an open bus slot.

4. Close the case.

5. Plug in the power cord, and turn the computer on.

6. Follow the manufacturer's directions on installing the device drivers for the NIC.

If you are using an external NIC, steps 1 through 5 are replaced by connecting a supplied cable from the NIC to either a USB port or the device's parallel port, depending on the type of NIC.

Once the NIC is installed, use a cable with RJ-45 connectors on each end to hook it to the jack.

2 Run a Network over Your Phone Lines

The telephone lines already in your home can provide a terrific approach to installing a home network. Because many—if not most—rooms in a home will have a telephone jack, you have a ready-made network, waiting only for special NICs that can take advantage of the wiring.

Phone-line networks are possible because all the extensions on a single phone line in a building are connected, as the diagram below shows. Using special NICs, you connect your computers to the phone jacks.

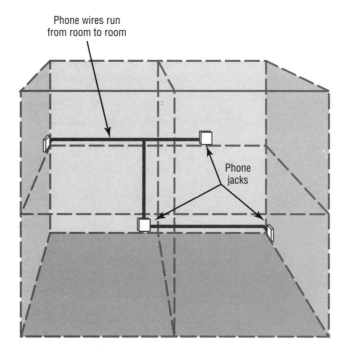

Phone wires run from room to room

Phone jacks

Phone wire with regular telephone connectors (type RJ-11) on each end connect a NIC to the telephone jack. Because the network operates at a different electrical frequency than telephones, the two can coexist on the same lines.

Phone Line Network Pros and Cons

The best reason to use phone networking is that it's easy. The phone wires are already in place; all you do is install the NICs and connect them to phone jacks. The Home Phoneline Networking Alliance (HomePNA) has defined standards for phone-line networks. Theoretically, equipment from one vendor should work with the hardware from another.

NOTE Most phone network equipment is available for Windows machines. Farallon's products support some Macintosh models, though older computers will not be supported.

NOTE Phone-line network capacities should be up to 10Mbps—or the low end of standard Ethernet speeds—by the time you read this. Because the telephone and network signals do not interfere with each other, you can take a telephone call while the network is running.

There are limitations to telephone networking, though. Each device on the network must be near a telephone jack, which means that the number and location of appropriate jacks limit your network. You could add telephone cables throughout the house, but it would be just as easy to run UTP cable.

There are also distance restrictions on the products. The ActionTec model, for example, restricts the farthest distance between any two computers up to 500 feet, which is shorter than the 200 meters, or almost 650 feet, possible with two UTP cables running to the same hub. For most homes, though, this should not be a problem. The main difficulty will be that you probably won't know the length of phone cord running inside the walls between jacks.

Install a Phone Line Network

Before installing hardware and software, give some thought to your phone lines. The network depends on all jacks being connected to the same phone line. If you have two or more separate phone lines, be sure the jacks you use are on the same line. Otherwise, it would be like getting a call at one phone number and picking up an extension on the other line.

You don't want to put in a phone network at the price of being unable to connect your phones. Check the NICs. Some come with two phone jacks, so you can connect the NIC to the phone jack and then plug the phone into the NIC and still use it.

NOTE If the NICs lack a second jack, buy some line splitters. These are little blocks that plug into a phone jack and turn it into two jacks, so you can plug in both the computer and the phone at the same time.

Installing the phone-line-network hardware is straightforward. Although these directions work with the ActionTec and Farallon products, others will be similar.

1. Turn off the computer, and unplug it.

2. Open the computer's case.

3. Find an open PCI slot, and insert the NIC.

4. Close the case again.

5. Take a cable, plug one end into the NIC and the other into the phone jack.

6. If the computer does not use a modem and you have a phone, plug it into the appropriate jack on the NIC. (Some products will require a splitter at the wall jack.)

7. If the computer uses either an internal or external modem, connect another phone cable from the phone jack on the NIC to the line jack on the modem. Then you can connect a phone to the modem's telephone jack.

8. Turn on the computer, and follow the manufacturer's instructions for installing the device drivers.

NOTE I used the phone network kits from ActionTec and Farallon, which include two NICs, two phone cables, and software for Windows 95, 98, or NT. Farallon's kit also supported Macs with open PCI slots.

ActionTec suggests unplugging any unused phones on the line, as excess equipment can cause electrical noise that can slow the network.

3 Run a Network over Your Power Lines

Mention running a network over power lines, and many people react as though advised to speed through their morning by using a hair drier while sitting in a warm tub. Fear not. Power-line networking is not only safe but often the only practical way of providing communications among your computers.

As the graphic below shows, power-line networks work because the power outlets in a building are all connected together. By using special equipment called *adapters,* the computers can send signals to each other through the house, turning the power lines into a network data transport mechanism.

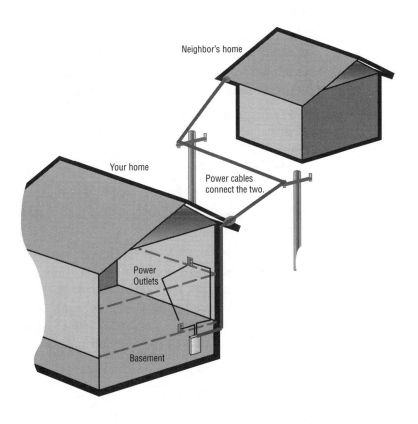

Neighbor's home

Your home

Power cables connect the two.

Power Outlets

Basement

Though the thought of plugging the back of a computer into an outlet may seem dangerous, it's not. Power-line networking uses special adapters, which are network devices that plug into wall outlets and connect with a cable to a computer's or printer's parallel port. The adapters are designed to keep power wiring physically separate from the cable running to the computer or printer, so there is no chance of damaging equipment or getting a shock. Because the network generates signals that are much different than household current, they can coexist without problems.

Power-Line Network Pros and Cons

Power-line networks have some clear advantages at home. There's no need for cutting holes in walls and pulling cable—an important issue if you rent an apartment or house. Virtually any place you might use a computer will have a power outlet, which means you can get connected.

Because the network devices are outside your computer, you don't have to install cards or open the PC. If you want to move the location of a computer, instead of running more network cabling, just unplug the power-line adapter and bring it with you.

There are also some drawbacks. The technology is recent and focused on the largest computing markets, which means Windows 95, 98, and NT. Depending on the product vendor, you are out of luck if you use Macs, earlier versions of Windows, Linux, or other platforms.

This form of network has the lowest bandwidth of any network, which means you are more limited in the amount of data that can travel over the network, and you may find it slower than most other types of networking technologies.

You might also start running out of wall outlets faster than before: some outlets may not work because of electrical interference. Power-line networks can be finicky.

Even with the potential problems, power-line networking is a great solution for many people. You can share files and printers, devices connected to PCs on the network, and even Internet access. It's easy to add a network connection anyplace you suddenly decide you want another connection, even if it's temporary. For example, on a hot day you could set up a network and move from a hot office to an air-conditioned bedroom in under an hour.

Install a Power-Line Network

The mechanics of putting in a power-line network are easy, as the following steps show:

1. Turn off the PCs and the printer.

2. Unplug the power cables of the PCs, and connect them to power conditioners, which are power strips that filter out any power-line noise that could disrupt the network. Then plug the power conditioner into the power outlet.

3. Plug the network adapters into power outlets, and connect parallel cables from the adapter to a computer or printer. There are two types of adapters, one for a computer and one for a printer, so be sure you don't mix them up.

4. Turn the PCs and printer back on.

5. Use the CD to install the software for the computers. The CD will configure Windows networking for you.

6. Be sure that drivers for the printer are installed on all the PCs that will use the printer.

NOTE I used Intelogis's PassPort power-line networking kit, which works with Windows 95/98 and Windows NT. This kit comes with two adapters for PCs, two parallel cables, one printer adapter, a CD with software and drivers, and two power-line conditioners. Similar products available from other vendors may be compatible with other operating systems.

You can add PCs and printers to the network with a few restrictions. There may be a limit on the total number of devices you can have in a network; for PassPort, the maximum number is 20. Also, printers using *bidirectional* communications—where they send signals to a PC over the printer cable as well as receive printing jobs—don't work on PassPort and may not on similar products. You can get around this by disabling bidirectional communications as follows:

1. Either choose a PC with at least two parallel ports or add a parallel port card to one of the computers.

2. Plug the printer into the second parallel port. If the printer must be on LPT1, you can move the network adapter to the second parallel port.

3. Double-click on Printers in My Computer on the Windows desktop.

4. Highlight the printer in question.

5. Click the right mouse button, and select Properties.

6. Uncheck the bidirectional box.

NOTE For more information about Windows networking, see "9. Set Up the Network Software" later in this part.

Set Up a Secure Power-Line Network

It is also a good idea to create a *secure* network, which means that only the specified machines can use that network. This is important with power-line networks because the wires in one house or apartment are connected to those of neighboring units. Without secure networks, someone next door using equivalent equipment might be able to get access to the machines on your network.

With the PassPort product, setting up a secure network is easy. Bring up the PassPort Administrator program on one of the networked PCs, choose Security from the menu, and then click on Secure Network Wizard. The program will walk you through the steps of choosing a network name and then picking the PCs and printers that are in it.

NOTE At the time of this writing, Intelogis had version 1 of PassPort. The company expects the maximum bandwidth in version 2 to almost triple to 1 million bits per second. The company was also considering support for other platforms.

4 Run a Network through the Air

An ideal network would be one in which you didn't have to connect anything, the data flying of its own accord where it had to go. That may be unrealistic, but wireless networks come close.

Rather than using cable, phone lines, or power lines, wireless networks rely on high-frequency radio transmissions. Instead of connecting to a wall jack or outlet, the NIC in a PC has a small protuberance that juts out of the computer's case. This is an antenna through which the NIC signals other units in the building. Because the radio signals are so high frequency—around 2.4 gigahertz, to be exact—the NICs are unlikely to clash with other household signals or broadcast transmissions.

Wireless Network Pros and Cons

The advantages of wireless networks are clear. There is less equipment to install and no wires to run. You can up and move a computer at any time without thinking about adjusting the network.

Because the signals are low power to avoid interference, they have a relatively short range of about 300 feet. You can get support for PCs running Windows 95 and 98, but wireless networking may not be available for other operating systems. Although wireless products claim between 1 to 2 megabits per second in transmission speed, experience suggests actual speeds of about half of that. However, by the time you read this, it is likely you will be able to find wireless products that operate at 10 megabits per second or more.

Install a Wireless Network

Because of the lack of cabling, wireless equipment is easy to install. Just follow these simple steps:

1. Turn off the PC, and unplug it.
2. Remove the PC's case.

3. Select an open PCI slot, and install the card.

4. Close the case, plug the PC in, and turn it on.

5. Install the software, according to the manufacturer's instructions.

NOTE   I used a wireless PCI card and a laptop PC card from Alation Systems. Because the company licenses the technology, you can find it under other company names, such as Diamond Multimedia.

5 Connect Older Computers to Your Home Network

It can be irritating to look at the newest network technologies and see they demand a minimum of Windows 95, when one of your PCs runs Windows 3.1. There's no reason to give up on the idea of networking older or supposedly obsolete computers. You can have a network with PCs running any version of Windows. In fact, you can network DOS machines.

The advantage is that you use computers you already own. Older computers can perform many tasks, such as

◆ Run a Linux Web server.

◆ Control special equipment, such as home-security devices or a home appliances.

◆ Use remote control to run applications in partnership with more modern machines.

NOTE   See "20. Find Uses for Old Computers," for more information.

Supporting older PCs on a network is not difficult. First you have to pick the network operating system. Then you choose the hardware and connect the PCs to your Ethernet network.

Pick the Platform

To create a network with older computers, first consider the network operating system. Just as a PC needs an operating system like Windows 3.1 or Windows 98 to run, so does a computer network. What gets confusing is that some PC operating systems have built-in network support; for example, a group of Windows NT Workstations, 98, and 95 computers work together on a network.

Unfortunately, Windows 95's and 98's built-in peer-to-peer networking doesn't support older PC operating systems such as Windows 3.1 or DOS. This means that if you want to network older operating systems with newer ones, you need to choose network software that will let all of your computers run together.

TABLE 5.1

Network Operating System	PC Platform		
	DOS	**Windows 3.11**	**Windows 3.1**
Windows NT Server	X	X	X
Windows 95/98; Windows NT Workstation	--	--	--
NetWare	X	X	X
Linux	X	X	X
LANtastic	X	X	X

Windows NT, Windows 2000, and NetWare are all powerful network operating systems but have significant disadvantages in cost and complexity.

Linux, which is available for free, fares better on expense but requires attentiveness and some degree of patience.

> **NOTE** Because each of these operating systems has its own complexities, a complete explanation is beyond the scope of this book. For more information, see *Mastering Local Area Networks*, by Christa Anderson and Mark Minasi (Sybex, 1999).

Notice the table mentions LANtastic, a peer-to-peer network operating system made by Artisoft (www.artisoft.com). Its strength is that you can connect PCs running DOS or any version of Windows, from 3.0 to 98 and even NT, both workstations and servers. You can configure LANtastic to run peer-to-peer, which means that all the PCs share resources, or have it use a central server. It has traditionally been easy to install and use.

Choose the Network Hardware

Once you have picked the network operating system, it's time to choose the hardware. Newer approaches to networking—phone lines, power lines, and radio transmission—support only newer systems, so plan on installing Ethernet UTP cable.

The NICs you choose must be compatible with the design of your PCs. Older hardware probably has an ISA bus, so you have two choices. One is to find an ISA internal NIC, which may be 8- or 16-bits, depending on your system. The other choice is an external NIC connecting to the parallel port, which is a slow solution.

Furthermore, NICs must also be compatible with your network operating system. This is another area that gets confusing when the operating system for the individual computers is the same as the network operating system. A NIC has to support *both* the PC's operating system *and* the network operating system. For example, Windows 98 has networking built in, so a vendor that says its NIC supports Windows 98 really means the networking portion. At the same time, a card that explicitly supports NetWare should support Windows 3.1—and DOS, for that matter—because NetWare has software for those platforms.

NOTE NetGear has a NIC that will work with either 8-bit or 16-bit ISA slots and that supports Windows for Workgroups 3.11, any version of Windows NT from 3.1 on, Windows 95/98, NetWare, Unix networks, LANtastic, and IBM's OS/2 server.

Unfortunately, installing NICs on older computers is more painful than with the plug-and-play cards available for Windows 95, 98, and NT. You inevitably have to configure each card. If you are lucky, this can be done with software. Otherwise, expect to set DIP switches or jumpers.

DIP switches are tiny slide switches mounted on the card. Using the tip of a ball-point pen, or some similar object, you move the switches to on or off positions. Jumpers are small connectors that fit over metal pins, connecting pairs of wires. Carefully follow the manufacturer's instructions for setting the *interrupts* (IRQs) and *addresses* for the card. It's not so important what these terms mean as that they are wild animals that must be satisfied. It's likely you will have to experiment with different settings to find what works for your system. A safe IRQ to use is typically number 10.

Dip switches

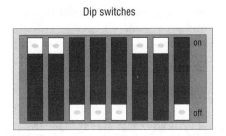

Jumpers

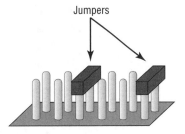

6 Connect a Mac to Your Home Network

Networking with PCs can be frustrating for Macintosh users. This isn't because of technical problems, but because most companies developing new networking technologies focus on PCs and Windows and ignore the needs of Mac users. Despite the slights—which are probably expected by Mac enthusiasts at this point—it is possible to connect both Macs and PCs to your home network. This allows them to share files, hard drives, and printers.

WARNING If using both PCs and Macs together, remember that each has different file formats that may not be compatible. Although JPEG graphics files are the same on both, TIFF graphics are slightly different. Even files produced by the same application on both platforms may not be compatible. For example, Microsoft Word for Macintosh files can't be read by Word for Windows unless you have installed the translator.

NOTE Macs can read diskettes formatted by Windows, but the opposite is not true. For those cases in which you have something on a Mac-formatted floppy or removable media, such as Zip or SyQuest, consider using MacDrive98 from Media 4 Productions. It allows a Windows 98 PC to read Macintosh media. However, it doesn't translate the files, so your applications will have to do that. There is an evaluation version of MacDrive98 on the CD accompanying this book. Install the program either automatically with the user interface on the CD or manually by double-clicking the file MacDrive98 Trial Version 3.1.2 Setup.exe in the directory \Put Networks in Place\MacDrive98\ on the CD.

Choose the Appropriate Cabling Scheme

You have two choices for mixing Macs and PCs on a network. One is to use phone-line networking. (See the section "2. Run a Network over Your Phone Lines.") Farallon has a Mac-compatible system.

NOTE By the time you read this, you should have a choice of either PCI cards, which will only work with newer Macs, or an external NIC.

Your other choice is the standard Ethernet cable route. Current Macs have Ethernet cards with RJ-45 jacks built-in, saving a lot of headaches. Some older Macs have an Ethernet card that requires an adapter with an RJ-45 jack before you can connect it to your UTP cable.

If you have to install a card for either a phone line or Ethernet network, the process is easy.

1. Turn off the Mac, and unplug it.

2. Open the case.

3. Insert the card in an open slot.

4. Close the case, plug the Mac in, and start it.

5. Follow the manufacturer's instructions for installing the device drivers.

Use PC MACLAN to Get the Mac and Windows Computers to Talk

Once you have the proper hardware, there's no need for bright lights and the third degree to get a Macintosh to talk to your PC network. Perhaps the easiest option to use for mixing PCs and Macs is to create a peer-to-peer network with both Macs and Windows PCs using a third-party product, such as PC MACLAN from Miramar Systems (www.miramarsys.com).

PC MACLAN runs on the PCs connected to your network; you don't need to install anything on the Macs. The Macs appear as icons in the Windows Network Neighborhood, while the PCs are available on a Mac's Chooser or Network Browser. The product allows you to share files and printers. It works using Apple's AppleTalk networking protocol. PC MACLAN adds a version of AppleTalk to a Windows computer.

There are versions of PC MACLAN for both Windows 95/98 and NT. Another Miramar product, Personal MACLAN Connect, provides peer-to-peer file and print sharing for Macs and Windows 3.0, 3.1, and 3.11.

NOTE The CD accompanying this book includes demo versions of both the Windows 95/98 and NT versions of PC MACLAN and the product documentation as well as a free copy of Personal MACLAN Connect. The demo versions will only run for three hours at a time, but they should help you decide whether you like the product.

To install PC MACLAN, follow these steps:

1. If you have a previous version of PC MACLAN installed, uninstall it first. If you use an antivirus utility, turn it off during this installation.

2. Install the program with the user interface on the CD accompanying this book, or install manually by double-clicking the file pcm72.exe in the directory \Put Network in Place\Pcmclan\ on the CD.

3. Open the Windows Explorer, highlight pcm72.exe, and double-click it.

4. Click OK when the virus protection window opens.

5. Choose Standard Installation, and click Continue.

6. Enter your name in the Enter User Information window, leave the other spaces blank, and click OK.

7. When asked to view changes, click No.

8. Click OK twice.

9. Click OK again. Ignore the note about not removing the installation disk.

10. Click Yes to restart your computer.

Copy the file PC_MACLAN_v7.2_Manual from the \Put Network in Place\ Pcmclan\ directory on this book's CD to your hard drive. This is the documentation. Follow the directions for configuring the software. You now have a network that works with both your PCs and your Macs.

NOTE You have three other options for mixing Macs and PCs on a single network. First, you can use AppleShare to connect to Windows computers, so by setting a Mac as a central server, your Windows 95 and 98 computers will have access to the drives and printers. You will need to install a special client—available from Apple—on the PCs to let them recognize the Mac server. Apple-Share is not cheap, however. A second approach is to use Windows NT Server, Novell NetWare, or Linux as a central server. All three will support both Macintosh and Windows machines, providing access to drives and printers. This method, however, will require more maintenance and a complex setup. A final approach is to use Dave, from Thursby Systems, which runs on the Macs on your network. It runs on Macs and makes them compatible with a Windows peer-to-peer network.

7 Mix Home Networking Technologies

Given the descriptions in earlier sections, you might think that networks and country clubs had exclusivity in common. That isn't true at all. You can set up multiple networks at the same time, each acting independently. Here are some examples of what is possible with more than one network:

◆ Creating a network to temporarily work from a different location

◆ Keeping a business network separate from household network uses

◆ Connecting a computer until you expand your cable network

You create more than one network by installing multiple NICs on some computers. The NICs are of different types, such as 10/100BaseT Ethernet and phone line. Because the different systems often can't communicate with each other, the result can be separate networks.

NOTE Zoom Telephonics has wireless products with special software that can connect the wireless network to an Ethernet network.

Decide on the Proportions

Before opening computer cases and plugging in NICs, take a moment to plan what you want to do and why. In general, it makes sense to have a general-purpose network connecting most of the network devices and a small one serving a special purpose. For example, the minor network might have only two PCs on it, while the main network would have all but one of your PCs as well as all of the printers.

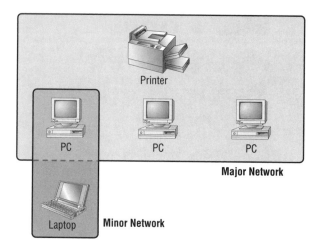

In the illustration above, the main network runs on Ethernet. The smaller network connects a laptop to the office computer with a wireless link.

There may be times, however, that you will want files from one network to be available on the other. One way to do this is place a machine acting as a server on both networks. So long as the files you need are on that computer, they will be available, no matter which network you are on.

You can also create a transfer directory. Take a computer that is on both networks, create a directory or folder, and call it *Transfer*. Be sure that both networks have read and write access to the directory. (See "9. Set Up the Network Software.") Put files into that directory when you want to move them between the networks.

8 Devise Great Locations for Network Connections

It's easy to make assumptions about home networks. One of the most limiting is that computers can belong only in certain rooms, such as a den or an office. But with a little thought, you may realize that there are many other places you might want a computer—if not permanently, then at least for part of the time. The network is there to help you, so be creative.

Let your network bring computing power to where you want it. Say, for example, that you are working at home. Then you might as well enjoy all the benefits. If the weather is nice, extend a network to a porch or a deck. With a wireless network, it is easy to improvise. (See "4. Run a Network through the Air.")

Using weatherproof covers, you can also run power, telephone, and some Ethernet cables to outside outlets. That way, your outside office is connected to the whole network, giving you access to everything.

Because there are many uses for a computer network, including distributing audio and video, another prime location is a playroom or spot near a treadmill. Not only can you listen to your favorite music or watch a DVD movie but there is also software to help monitor exercising. (See the part "Use Your Network to Deliver Entertainment.")

Other possible locations include the kitchen, where access to your DVD library can bring you cooking shows. Other networked kitchen aides include a computer database for recipe management and project-management software to plan preparation for a large dinner party. (See sections "68. Let Everyone Use the Same Shopping and To-Do Lists," and "70. Automate Your Meals with a Kitchen Network Center.").

Having a networked computer in your garage might also be handy. For instance, you could store vehicle maintenance records on your network as well as provide a place to check your to-do list when doing yard work.

Remember, the only real restriction on where you can have a computer is the need for an electrical outlet.

9 Set Up the Network Software

You've got the network hardware hooked together, so you're ready to "network," right? Not so fast.

As a PC needs an operating system to run, so does a network. Without the software, the network is nothing more than a bunch of boxes strung together with phone cord. It's the network operating system or NOS, that makes communications and sharing network resources possible.

It's a good thing that getting your NOS ready can be easy. Here are the overall steps you have to take:

1. Choose the NOS you will use on your network.

2. Decide on user access to the network.

3. Create unique identities for the computers.

4. Create unique identities for the users.

5. Set permissions for network access, which means implementing the decisions you made in step 2.

Once these steps are complete, you'll be ready to share files and devices across your network.

Choose Your NOS

Picking the network operating system is critical, if for no other reason than that you invest time setting it up and then have to live with it. There are two basic NOS types you can choose from: client/server and peer-to-peer.

A client/server NOS is probably what most people think of as a network. There's a central machine, called a *server,* that controls the network's operations. Each PC connects to the server, which performs services on that computer's behalf. Some of the common client/server NOSs are

◆ Windows NT Server

◆ Windows 2000 Server

◆ Novell NetWare

◆ Linux

Client/server network operating systems let you efficiently share files, printers, equipment, and even Internet access. You have excellent control over who has access to what data or devices, and you can even set up your own Web server. A client/server NOS, however, tends to be complex to configure and maintain, and you typically have to "tune" them, like a car, to get the best performance. Other than Linux, they are also expensive, costing hundreds of dollars or more for a small installation.

The other type of NOS is the peer-to-peer. Instead of a central computer that controls the network, each PC lends a hand, making its own hard drives, printers, and CD drives available to the other systems on the network.

They aren't as fast or powerful as client/server network operating systems, but peer-to-peer network packages are relatively easy to configure and use. And because most computers in your house are already running either Windows 95 or Windows 98—which both have built-in peer-to-peer networking capabilities—this section will concentrate on them.

NOTE If you want more information on working with a client/server NOS, check out *Mastering Local Area Networks,* by Christa Anderson and Mark Minasi (Sybex, 1999), or *Mastering Linux Premium Edition,* by Arman Danesh (Sybex, 1999), which includes eight chapters on using Linux in a small office/ home setup. It also includes a copy of Linux.

Decide on User Access to the Network

You might think that deciding on what people in your household can use on the network is a waste of time. After all, shouldn't everyone be able to use everything? If your home is like most others, the answer is no. Here are some examples:

◆ Parents want to keep children from surfing the Web when they are out of the house.

◆ One person in an apartment is concerned that roommates accidentally change or erase important work-related files.

◆ You configured a particular program to your liking and don't want someone else to change it.

To decide on user access, you need to create an access plan. Here are the steps that will result in one:

1. Draw a matrix on paper with the names of people in your home written across the top and the network devices you have down the left side.

2. Write an "X" in at the intersection of a person and a device if the person should be able to use the device.

3. Draw another matrix with the names of people down the left side and the names of files and directories across the top. This will cover access to the files and directories.

4. At the intersection of a person and a file or directory, write *R* if a person should be able to read the file or directory; *W* for writing, changing, or deleting files; *X* to run a program; or *M* to modify access for others. As an example, if someone should be able to read or write a file, you would write *RW*.

Not only do you have a framework for deciding high-level access questions, but you also have the subtleties of the *type* of access each person has.

TABLE 9.1   Device Access Worksheet

	Office Computer C: Drive	Sun Room Computer E: Drive
Richard	RWX	RW
Mary	RWXM	–
Danilo	RW	RX
Deb	R	RWXM

Access is hierarchical, which means that if one directory contains another, then the first directory's access settings can take precedence. For example, if the Photos directory is within the Documents directory, you can't give someone write access to Photos without giving them write access to Documents. However, someone could have write access to Documents while having read-only access to Photos. So you need to plan access with an eye on directory structure.

Because of the nature of Windows peer-to-peer networking, there is less access control than in client/server networks. Your choice is to give someone read-only access or full access, which includes read, write, execute, and modify. So we have to modify our plan somewhat, as the next table shows.

TABLE 9.2 Permissions Level Worksheet

	Office Computer C: Drive	Sun Room Computer E: Drive
Richard	Full	Read Only
Mary	Full	None
Danilo	Read Only	Full
Deb	Read Only	Full

To change access levels, right-click on the Folder, and select Sharing. Select Shared As:. Under Access Type:, select the type of access, which is either Read-Only or Full.

Soon we will associate access levels with passwords. This is not as secure a method as a corporation might want, but it should be fine for home use.

Once you have your lists, go into the network operating system, and set the access accordingly. For instance, you can give everyone read-only access to the file networkplans.doc in C: under Windows 98 easily by changing access to either the file or the directory.

Create Identities for the Computers

For now, though, we will wait on doing anything else with the access plans. First we will create identities for the computers. In Windows networking, that involves both an individual machine name and a *workgroup* name. The workgroup is just a collection of PCs that will work with one another on the network. You would typically put all your PCs in the same workgroup at home. The machine name is a unique name (limited to 15 characters) that identifies a particular PC, such as Office or Kitchen.

Say, for example, that you want to call the computer in your den Work and have it as part of the Home workgroup. Here's how you would do that in Windows 98:

1. Highlight Network Neighborhood on your desktop.

2. Right-click, and choose Properties.

3. Select the Identification tab.

4. Type in the computer name and workgroup.

5. While it's not necessary, you can add a description of what the computer does.

6. Click OK.

You have set the identity for that one PC. Now you have to do the same thing for every PC on the network.

WARNING Be sure to be consistent in the spelling of the workgroup name. Only computers with *exactly* the same workgroup name can communicate under Windows networking.

Create Identities for the Users

Most client/server networks and Windows peer-to-peer networking differ in an important respect: client-server networks require that each person who accesses the network have a separate network identity. Network operating systems require this identity because there is a basic flaw in setting network security by machine names: You have no guarantee that a person using a particular PC is that machine's owner. Managing these individual identities—or accounts—can be difficult. Fortunately, home networking usually does not require this level of control.

If you are using Windows 95/98 peer-to-peer networking, you don't have to worry about setting up individual user accounts. Windows 98 supports user identities only when connected to a Windows NT server or Novell Net-Ware system. So our configuration won't use this.

Set Permissions for Network Access

Remember that in the second part of step two, you modified the access lists to account for Windows networking? Now it's time to implement these permissions. Taking the example of the Office computer, there will be a password, called *total*, that provides full access. Another password, called *limited*, provides read-only access.

Here are the steps you would take to implement those passwords:

1. Go into My Desktop of the Office computer, and highlight the C: drive.

2. Right-click, and choose Sharing.

3. Select Shared As.

4. Select Depends on Password under Access Type.

5. Type the word **total** in the Full Access Password.

6. Type the word **limited** in the Read-Only Password.

7. Click OK.

Notice that you could have chosen to give everyone on other machines either Read-Only or Full Access by appropriately choosing the Access Type.

Now your network is read to use. The rest of the book provides ideas for useful and fun things you can do with the network.

Get Your Network to Work for You

There are many things a network can do for you—just look at the examples throughout the rest of this book. But some of the biggest benefits you will see come from networking fundamentals, such as

- ◆ Get access to an important file, no matter where you are in your home.

- ◆ Have one copy of an application that multiple people can use, without taking up hard-drive space on each computer.

- ◆ Protect all your PCs from viruses at the same time.

- ◆ Check if the network is working correctly.

- ◆ Find problems with hard drives *before* they crash and you lose important information.

Network basics not only provide lots of benefits, they also make everything else you do with a network possible.

10 Share Files on the Network

Saying that networks let you share files seems obvious, but sometimes the obvious is cool. By making it possible to share files, a network lets you

- ◆ Buy one copy of an application, and let everyone run it.

- ◆ Maintain a work-and-play schedule for multiple people.

- ◆ Have a single phone list that the whole family shares.

- ◆ Play music from any location from a central music server.

- ◆ Work on an important document from any location on the network, inside or outside.

All this is possible because networks let computers share their files, whether they are programs, music, phone lists, or images.

You have two considerations in file sharing: where to put the files and how to get access to them.

Designate a File Server

Choosing where to put the files depends on the type of network operating system you have and how you have set it up. Remember, there are two basic types of networks: client/server, where a single computer controls the network, and peer-to-peer, where all the PCs cooperate to control the network. Whichever you use, you can share files.

In a client/server network, files typically reside on the same computer running the NOS. That's because it is the only computer to whose hard drives the other PCs have access. This machine is called the *file server,* because it becomes a central repository of files and "serves 'em up" to the other computers.

In a peer-to-peer network, you can make a hard drive on any networked computer available to others. Yet you should still plan on thinking in terms of file servers. The reason is really organizational.

Having many drives available to you on a network becomes a potential problem if you actually use them, because you suddenly need to track which files are kept on what machine. Have you ever forgotten where you put a file on a single hard drive? Try looking on five. When you designate one computer as the file server, you know where to check.

Given the nature of home networks, you don't need to use the most powerful PC in the house for a file server. A more modest computer will do well. That may seem surprising. Corporations often favor fabulously fast machines, but that's because they have important applications running on the servers that all the employee's use. Because you are looking to provide file access, speed of the CPU is less important.

Make Sure There's Enough Memory

For file sharing, CPU muscle is more important than memory. You don't need hundreds of megabytes of RAM, but 32MB is good, and 64MB is better.

NOTE   RAM memory is fairly inexpensive. Consider upgrading the memory of your file server from the 16MB or 32MB it had when you bought it to a more robust 64MB.

Make sure that the hard drive is large, which, depending on your situation and what you do with the computers, might mean 10 to 20 gigabytes. That may sound like a lot, but as you start storing multimedia files, especially audio and video, you will find it disappearing in no time.

NOTE   I turned a 120MHz, AMD-powered PC with 32MB of memory into a good file server by adding a 10.2GB Quantum Fireball hard drive.

Make Sure There's Enough Storage Space

You may decide that you don't have enough hard-drive space. Instead of buying a new computer, why not add another hard drive to your old one? Here's how to do it:

1. Turn off your computer, unplug it, and then open the case.

2. Check that there is an open *drive bay*. This is the part of the PC chassis that actually holds a hard drive in place.

3. Most computers in the home will have an IDE drive, which means it connects to the computer with a ribbon cable terminated by a connector that has 40 holes in the end, as the following drawing shows. Another connector with four holes in the end provides the power. Your computer's manufacturer can tell you what sort of drive it has. When buying a new drive, you need to get the same type. One exception is when adding a SCSI drive to a PC. This section discusses SCSI drives later.

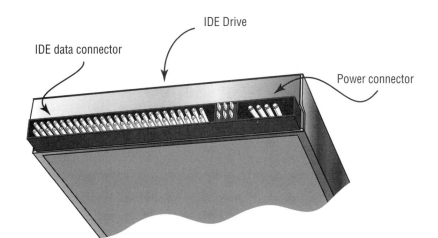

IDE Drive

IDE data connector

Power connector

....

NOTE There are two types of bays in your computer: a 5.25-inch size and a 3.5-inch size. Hard drives are typically 3.5-inch. If you only have a 5.25-inch open bay, purchase a set of *rails*. These metal attachments hold the hard drive in the larger space.

4. Because you are adding the additional hard drive, you will need to configure the drive, probably by moving jumpers on the unit, to act as a *slave* to the original drive. See the directions that come with the hard drive for how to do this.

5. Slide the drive into the bay, and use four screws to hold it in place.

....

WARNING Only use screws intended for mounting hard drives. Too long a screw could poke through the mounting rail, touch electrical circuitry, and damage the drive.

6. The ribbon cable running to the first hard drive should have a second connector. Attach it to the new hard drive, and then attach a spare power connector.

7. Close the case, plug the PC in, and turn it on.

8. You now need to configure the BIOS to recognize the new drive. As your computer boots up, follow the instructions on the screen for how to start "setup." You should note that the menus on different BIOSes may vary. With an AMI BIOS, for example, the first menu item of Standard CMOS contains the hard-drive configuration information. If your BIOS contains an Auto Detect feature, run Auto Detect, and ensure the new drive has been detected. If detected properly, Save your settings and exit BIOS.

9. Look for the spot to configure the primary slave hard drive. If your PC and hard drive are both "plug-and-play," set the hard-drive type to Auto. Otherwise, set the hard-drive type of User, and enter the number of cylinders, sectors, and heads, provided in the information from the hard drive's vendor.

10. Follow the on-screen instructions to save the new BIOS values, and then let the machine restart.

WARNING   If your server is an older PC, the BIOS may not support a large hard drive. In that case, you need a copy of Disk Manager DiskGo! by Ontrack (www.ontrack.com). It adds a special driver that will overcome the BIOS limitations and let an older machine use drives larger than two gigabytes.

11. You now have to format and partition the hard drive. *Partitions* are logical divisions within the hard drive. It is necessary to partition a hard drive because operating systems have limitations on the amount of contiguous hard-drive space they can recognize. You can partition and format the drive with the MS-DOS command called *fdisk,* but Partition Magic from PowerQuest Corporation (www.powerquest.com) will also do the job and requires less knowledge and patience to partition. It graphically walks you through the process.

Add a SCSI Drive

If additional people in your home need access to large files, consider adding a SCSI drive. SCSI, or Small Computer System Interface, is a standard type of computer interface for many devices, including hard drives, CD-ROM drives, and scanners. Although more expensive than an IDE drive, a SCSI hard drive can run many times faster than the more usual IDE hard drive.

To run a SCSI drive, you need a SCSI interface card. This fits into the server the way any other add-in card would. To install the card, use this procedure:

1. Turn off the PC, and unplug it.

2. Open the PC's case.

3. Find an open slot, and insert the card.

4. Follow the vendor's directions for connecting cables from the SCSI hard drive to the interface card.

5. Close the case, plug the PC in, and turn it on.

6. Follow the vendor's installation directions to load a SCSI driver.

7. As with IDE drives, you have to format and partition the hard drive. You can do this with the MS-DOS command called *fdisk,* but Partition Magic from PowerQuest Corporation (www.powerquest.com) makes the job easier.

Whether you have a client/server or peer-to-peer network, once you have selected the file server and added additional hard-drive space, if necessary, the next step to sharing files is to make sure different computers on the network have access to the server's drives. (See "9. Set Up the Network Software.") But setting the access depends on what you want to accomplish.

NOTE Instead of adding hard drives and converting older machines, you could also buy a new computer. With the way prices have plummeted, consumer model PCs can come with lots of horsepower. I tried a Presario from Compaq that came with 64 megabytes of RAM as well as a 466MHz Intel Celeron processor. This should be fast enough for almost anything you will want to do. Another choice could be special hard drives that connect directly to your network, keeping you from opening the PC or even wondering what partitions are.

Plan File Access

Once you know where files are going to be, you should plan what you want to share. Look at the different file types you might want to keep on your network. They might include word processing, spreadsheets, graphics, video, and audio files. Don't consider programs and utilities at this time, as the section "11. Share Applications across the Network" covers those topics. And unlike the section "9. Set Up the Network Software," in which you set general permissions for different directories, this section shows when to focus on individual files. Remember, though, that it does no good to place a shared file in a directory other people can't read.

First, decide who should be able to use the files. You might, for instance, let everyone have access to scanned photos or pictures taken with a digital camera but only allow yourself access to work-related documents.

You may notice that the files break out according to type—in other words, perhaps all graphics files should be available to everyone, while you should be the only person opening spreadsheets. However, there are no hard and fast rules, only what works for your needs.

If you are using peer-to-peer networking and have decided against a single file server, decide where you want to store common files. Although not all your files would be on the same PC, it still makes sense to keep all files of one type together. Otherwise, you have to remember which PC contains the word-processing document you need or resign yourself to spending time browsing through directories on multiple machines.

Create a logical naming convention for directories. Having a Kids Pictures file listed under the Family Photos folder will help you rapidly narrow a search among all the graphics files. Similarly, long filenames under Windows or Macs let you provide descriptive titles. Use them to clearly indicate contents without forcing someone to open the file.

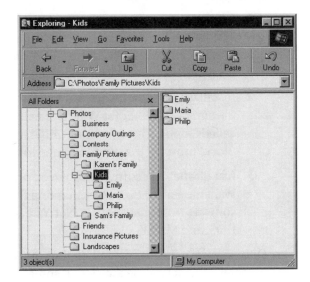

NOTE You don't have to give everyone access to everything. If a person in your home is the only one who uses certain files, you can create a folder on a shared drive and give only that person access. That will prevent anyone from accidentally tampering with the file's content.

Note that machines need direction to make drives and files available to others. You can restrict access as you wish. (See the section "9. Set Up the Network Software.") In fact, you will likely need to actively provide availability, as a NOS often restricts access as its default. Windows 98, for instance, initially makes drives read-only.

Access Files on a Client-Server Network

Setting up the file server is only half the battle. The other half is giving the PCs access to what is on a server. Although the details of different client/server network operating systems are too involved to cover here, there are some general steps to giving your PCs access:

1. Purchase whatever licenses you need. For example, owning a copy of Windows NT Server doesn't give you permission to connect a Windows 98 computer to it. In this case, you need to purchase a Windows NT Server Client Access License for each PC.

2. Install whatever software you need on the server. Linux can act as a file and print server for Windows machines if you run the program called Samba. This lets Linux understand the SMB (Server Message Block) protocol that Windows networking uses.

3. Install whatever software you need on the PCs. If you are using a NetWare file server, every computer on the network needs to run special software to connect with it. NetWare has client software for Windows, DOS, and MacOS.

Once you have finished installing the software, the PC clients should have access to your server. Be aware that some client/server network operating systems require the clients to log onto the network each time they power up. Without the logon, the people using the machines will have no access to files and directories.

Access Files on a Peer-to-Peer Network

On a peer-to-peer network, you map a network drive. This means you create an alias drive letter that your system will use in referring to networked directories. If you had two PCs, called Office and Laptop, on your network, you could make the C: drive on the Office machine appear as a different drive letter, say E:, on the Laptop machine. Under Windows 98, for example, you instruct your local PC to recognize a particular drive on the network:

1. Highlight, and then right-click the Network Neighborhood icon on the desktop.

2. Click on Map Network Drive.

3. The Drive list box at the top of the dialog box lets you pick the local drive letter to use. It will only show drive letters not currently in use.

4. The Path list box lets you pick or specify the network drive you want to map to the drive letter. Under Windows peer-to-peer networking, to specify the C: drive on the Office machine, you would type **\\Office\C**. You can only map a drive to a resource that is already shared. In this format, the C: drive is already shared.

5. Click OK.

The drive will now be available in all applications.

NOTE The software included with the network kit you use may set up drive mappings with a different interface. Follow the vendor's directions in such cases.

11 Share Applications across the Network

With a network, you can actually run applications that aren't even on your computer. That gives you some great advantages:

◆ If you need a particular application that is on a computer in use, you don't have to wait for the person using the computer to finish.

◆ Depending on how many computers require an application, you can save money with special network versions.

◆ An older computer can actually run an application by using the power of another PC.

There are some disadvantages, though. Installing software to run over the network can be a bit trickier than putting it on the machine you are using. If an older PC is using another PC to run an application, someone else can't use that PC. Also, running software over the network is slower than running it locally on a computer.

Given that, it's still good to know that you can put applications on the network if you need to.

When Can Software Be Networked?

When you start a program, the software loads into your computer's memory and then executes its encoded instructions. You might expect that you could start a program on a file server and then have the contents pass over the network to your computer to load into memory and run.

You would be right, at least sometimes. You can start some programs from a network location. However, there are many programs that, if you installed them on one machine and then tried to run them over the network from another PC, simply wouldn't work.

The problem is that while most applications do install into a special directory they create, they also add necessary files in other places, such as the System directory under Windows. So the directory named for the application—which you see over the network—contains only part of the program. Even if it is the vast majority, it is still missing critical files.

When you try to run the program over the network, it looks for the special files, but the application's installation routine loaded them onto the other PC. However, the program runs from the memory of the machine you used to start it, so it cannot find those files. Failing to find the files it needs, it informs you of the error and promptly stops. There is a way around this problem, though.

Here's how you can properly install a program on the network:

1. First, ask the vendor whether the program can run over the network.

2. Install the program on your file server.

3. If the vendor said the program can run over a network, you are set.

4. If the vendor didn't design the program to run over the network, decide which PCs you want to run the software.

5. Install the software on each of those PCs. When the software gives you the option to change the installation directory, choose the directory on the network drive you used to install the package on the server.

By following this procedure, even if an application doesn't normally run over the network, you have installed the special files on each machine you want to run the application.

....

WARNING You may not be allowed to install software on multiple machines or to let more than one person use it. Check "17. Stay Legal," for more information.

There is also software that comes in multiuser, or network, versions. This can mean two things. Strictly speaking, a software package that allows you to install it on multiple computers would be multiuser. Then there is a type of software you install on a network file server. More than one person, up to the number allowed by the manufacturer, can use the software at the same time. With such packages, you don't have to reinstall the program on every computer. Instead, the software is designed to reside completely on a file server, allowing other machines to run the program over the network. In some cases, however, you might have to install a small client subset of the program on each individual PC.

Versions for networks are typically cheaper than buying an equivalent number of single copies of an application. They also typically run slower, because some information required for the application has to be passed back and forth over the network, which is slower than having everything on one computer.

....

WARNING If you have both Macintosh and Windows computers on your network, you probably will not be able to share applications across the network between these platforms. Windows computers will not run Macintosh software, although some Macintosh computers have special software and hardware to run Windows applications.

Set Up a Faux Application Server with LapLink

Wouldn't it be nice to run a program that is sitting on another computer without having to install it on both machines? You can do that with an application server.

You may have heard the term before. It means that a computer on a network—a server—not only contains the files a program needs but actually runs the software on the behalf of another computer—the client. For those who like sports metaphors, it's the designated hitter of the software world.

The client performs only a small portion of the necessary work, such as running the user interface. A Web server is an example of an application server. Your computer runs the browser, which is the interface. The browser sends commands to the Web server, which performs some action and returns special HTML code that your browser displays.

Application servers are rarely easy to set up, and they typically require a client/server NOS. Luckily, there is a sneaky way around the problem—you can use remote control software. For example, LapLink, from Traveling Software, is often used for transferring files from one computer to another, and it is easy and convenient to install. However, LapLink can also let one PC take control of a second, which means it isn't as flexible as a real application server, because only one client can use the server at a time.

 Before arranging a computer coup d'etat, however, follow these instructions for installing LapLink Professional:

1. Double-click `Startup.exe` in the \Get Network to Work for You\LapLink\ directory on the CD accompanying this book. (You must install LapLink Pro manually through Windows Explorer. It *cannot* be installed from the `clickme.exe` interface.)

2. When the installation window opens, click Install Software Now!

Follow the on-screen instructions and you are ready to control on PC from another.

Here's how to set up a remote control session with LapLink:

1. Install LapLink on both computers. Call the one with the application the *Host* and the one you will use to start the application the *Guest*. These are LapLink's terms. You can think of them as the server and client, respectively.

2. Start LapLink on both computers.

3. On the Guest, click the Connect Over button on the toolbar, and choose Network.

4. Click the Available Now tab, and choose the Guest computer's name.

5. Choose Remote Control.

6. Press the Open Remote Control button.

You can now see what is on the Host's screen. Choose the application you want, and start it.

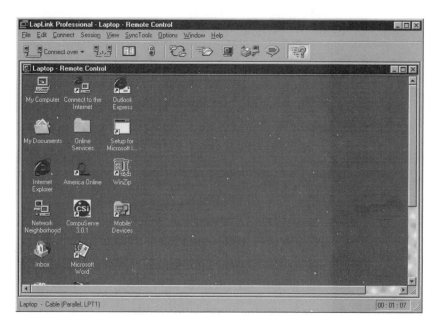

12   Share Devices across the Network

With a network, you can not only share files and applications but even devices such as

- ◆ Printers

◆ Modems

◆ CD-ROM and DVD-ROM drives

This is literally one of the biggest pay-offs for network users. For example, you can buy one printer for a group of people. There is also convenience. If you have an older black-and-white laser-jet printer attached to the PC you are using, you don't have to swap cables to use the photo-realistic printer connected to another computer.

Because of the number of network operating systems and the different ways they have of setting up device sharing, this section only discusses how to set up device sharing under Windows peer-to-peer networks.

Share a Printer

To share a printer requires only a few steps:

1. If you haven't already, enable File and Print sharing in Windows. (See "9. Set Up the Network Software.")

2. Select Start ➢ Settings ➢ Printers.

3. Highlight the icon of the printer you want to share.

4. Right-click, and select Properties.

5. Click the Sharing tab.

6. Select Shared As. Provide a unique name, up to 12 characters in length, and then click OK.

Now the printer is available to other PCs on the network.

Share a CD or DVD Drive

Because Windows treats a CD-ROM drive or DVD-ROM drive like a hard drive, you make them available the same way you would with a folder or file:

1. Open Windows Explorer or My Computer on the desktop.

2. Highlight the CD- or DVD-ROM drive.

3. On the File menu, click Properties.

4. Click the Sharing tab, and then click Shared As.

5. Provide a unique name, up to 12 characters in length.

6. Choose the Access Type you want, and provide passwords if you wish.

Now the drive is available to other systems on the network.

Share a Modem

Modems are a different animal. Windows isn't designed to share them on its own, so you need some additional software. There are two types of software you can use. One is called a proxy server and is used to share an Internet connection. Windows 98 Special Edition has a built-in proxy server. You can also get third party proxy servers for other versions of Windows. Check the section "36. Share Your Internet Connection over the Network" for more information.

The other type of software is a port-sharing application, such as SAPS from Spartacom Communications (`www.spartacom.com`). Unlike a proxy server, people on the network can make any use of the shared modem, from dialing the Internet to sending faxes.

With SAPS, both the server and the other PCs need to run special software. To install the product, first follow these steps for the server:

1. Install the program with the user interface on the CD accompanying this book, or install manually by double-clicking the file `setup.exe` in the directory \Get Network to Work for You\Saps\Server\ on the CD.

2. Click Next twice. Be sure Install SAPS Server and Its Manager is checked, and then click Next again.

3. Select Manage SAPS Servers for Windows 95 only, and then click Next.

4. You must provide an individual's name and a company name, and then click Next and Yes.

5. Click Next to accept the default directory, and then click Next to accept the program folder name.

6. Because this is an evaluation copy, click Next without entering a serial number or a key.

7. Click Finish and you are done with the installation.

You should see an open file with information on installation and usage as well as the SAPS Service Manager.

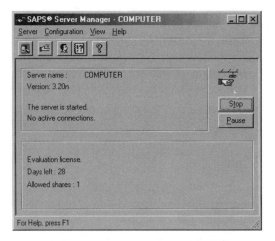

Next, you have to add a modem as a shared device:

1. Choose Shares from the Configuration menu on the Service Manager.

2. Click New.

3. Choose the port of the modem you want to share, type in the name you want to use under Share Name, and click Add.

4. Click OK twice.

Now you need to install the client program on all other PCs on your network. For each PC, follow these steps:

1. Install the program with the user interface on the CD accompanying this book, or install manually by double-clicking the file setup.exe in the directory \Get Network to Work for You\Saps\Client\ on the CD.

2. Click Next. Because this is an evaluation version, you will not have a serial number or a key, so click Next again.

3. Select Use a Pool of Network, and click Next.

4. Click Add, and enter the name of the port you entered in the server program.

5. Click OK, and then Next three times.

You can now share the network modem from this client.

13 Protect Your Network Files from Data Loss

Few sights are as pathetic as the face of people who have lost important information or files from their computer only to realize that they don't have copies. Luckily, a computer network gives you some terrific ways of avoiding the problem.

There are many ways you can lose files:

- ◆ You can accidentally delete them.

- ◆ You can uninstall software, including files needed by other programs.

- ◆ You can mistakenly overwrite a file, such as a word-processing document, with something else.

- ◆ You can sit helplessly as your computer crashes.

Whatever the cause, you are left sitting without something you want or need. It doesn't matter whether it is a file for work, a saved version of a computer game session in which you completed a difficult task, or your shopping list.

Undelete a Lost File with an Undelete Utility

Imagine accidentally deleting an important file and then emptying the Recycle Bin! If you catch the problem soon enough, you can always use an undelete utility.

An undelete utility actually goes into your hard drive and digs up a file whose space is now up for grabs. Programs such as FixIt Utilities 98 from Ontrack or Symantec's Norton Utilities have tools for recovering files emptied from a Windows recycle bin. Symantec also has a version of Norton Utilities for the Mac.

Because the operating system assumes it can overwrite a file once it's out of the recycle bin or trash can, time is of the essence. The sooner you try to recover the file, the more likely you will be successful.

Back Up Your Network Files on Offline Storage

Unhappily, there are many times when you just can't undelete a file. It's for those cases that you should back up your files. With copies of files and applications safely squirreled away somewhere, it is always possible to restore them if you need them.

You can also create *offline storage*, where you keep files you don't need on the network all the time, such as archived documents. Think of it as a backup you know you will need one day rather than backup for an emergency.

Backup on a network can actually be easy, because you can automate the whole process and have it happen in the middle of the night, when it won't interfere with anyone. All you have to do is pick the right hardware, configure the backup software, and let the network do the rest.

Pick the Hardware

There is a range of backup choices to satisfy any need or budget. Although you could choose from types that include optical storage and digital audio tape (DAT), there are two particularly good ones for the home network— cartridge tape drives and CD or DVD drives. Each has its own strengths and weaknesses.

Tape drives are great for backing up a lot of material in one place. You can have one tape that holds the content of your entire network. The ability to compress data provides even more capacity. The larger the capacity, however, the longer it takes to find a particular file when you want to restore it. Because a large capacity tape drive is a specialized item, you should need only one on the network.

Search times for a given file on a CD-ROM or DVD drive are far shorter. And because most computers on your network probably have a CD or DVD drive, if you want to restore a file to a particular machine, you can load it directly. But CDs and DVDs have limited capacity—about 600 megabytes for the former and a few gigabytes for the latter—which makes them more suitable for storing files offline. Look for a rewritable drive so you can reuse the disks and also add content over time, instead of having to record everything at one time.

NOTE I have used a Tecmar tape drive to back up my PC for the last two years and have just switched to a 20 gigabyte model that can handle all the data on my network. An HP CD-RW, which reads CDs at 24X speed and records CDs at 4X, is helping store scanned photographs without cluttering hard drives.

Pick the Software

To make a backup, you need software that can run your hardware. Tape drives typically come with backup software, but not all such applications are made the same. For instance, some software can work while people are using the network.

If you are using a client/server network product, you will probably need a network backup product. If the network is peer-to-peer, you might be able to get away with a regular backup package, such as Seagate Backup Exec, which is the full version of the backup software included in Windows 98. Be sure that the computer connected to the backup tape drive has full access to all the drives on all the PCs in your network.

While some backup software may be able to write to CDs or DVDs, you really need recording software to take best advantage of them. The drives usually come with such software.

Run the Backup

Now it's time to configure the actual backup job. This example uses VER-ITAS Backup Exec because it can schedule the jobs to run in the middle of the night. Before you start, you have to work out a backup schedule. The following works well with two tapes, one for complete backups and one to backup files that have changed:

◆ One day a week, say Sunday, you back up everything on the full-backup tape.

◆ On Monday, you erase the changed file backup tape and then back up only the files that have changed since the last full backup.

◆ On Tuesday through Saturday, you back up only files that have changed since the last full backup. These backups get added to the end of the tape you used Monday.

With this approach, you can re-create anything on your network within the last week and need only two tapes to do so.

To make this work, first configure access on the network so the machine with the tape drive has full access to all the hard drives on all of your PCs.

Here's how to create the Sunday job:

1. Click Start ➢ Accessories ➢ System Tools ➢ Backup.

2. Select Create a New Backup Job, and click OK.

3. Select Back Up Selected Files, Folders, and Drives, and click Next.

4. Check all the hard drives on the backup computer. Then click the plus sign next to Networks, and select all the other drives; then click Next.

5. Select All Selected Files, and click Next.

6. Select the tape drive, and click Next.

7. Make sure both the Compare Original and Backup Files and Compress the Backup Data to Save Space boxes are checked, and then click Next.

8. Type a name for the job, and click Start. Immediately click Cancel when the job starts.

9. Click Options.

10. Select the General tab, and be sure that Overwrite the Media with This Backup is selected.

11. Select the Report tab, and be sure that Perform an Unattended Backup is selected.

12. Select the Advanced tab, and be sure that Back Up Windows Registry is checked, and then click OK.

13. Click the Schedule button, and pick when to run the job.

14. Under the Job menu, select Save.

Now create the two jobs for Monday and the rest of the week. For both, you would select "New and Changed Files" in step 5. For the Tuesday through Saturday job, you would select "Append This Backup to My Media" in step 10.

Back Up Your Network Online

The problem with doing backups at home is that if anything happens to the tapes, you would be out of luck. Outside obvious acts of God, such as fire and tornadoes, pets, children, and accidents can render tapes useless.

For extra protection, consider using an online backup service. These companies let you upload backups over the Internet to their servers.

You won't want to back up everything on your system every night, but it's a great way of keeping your most vital records, information, and files someplace safe.

NOTE If your Internet account comes with storage space for a Web page, you could upload your most critical files there. Check with your ISP whether this would make them available to people on the Internet.

Restore Your Data

Should you lose a file and need to restore it, you will use the restore portion of the backup software. Aside from recovering from a data loss, though, you can perform other tasks with restore:

◆ Move large blocks of files and directories from one system to another.

◆ Load data you have moved to offline storage.

◆ Move a Windows Registry and files to make one system act like another.

Restoring data is as easy as backing it up in the first place. With Microsoft Backup, which comes with Windows, you do the following:

1. Click Start ➤ Programs ➤ Accessories ➤ System Tools, and select Backup.

2. Select Restore Backed Up Files, and click OK.

3. Follow the instructions in the wizard for selecting the files to restore and their destination.

Then all you have to do is wait for the files to be written to the hard drive you indicated.

14 Protect Your Home Network from Viruses with VirusNet

Using antivirus software is like doing backups: it is one of the smartest things that most computer users never do. A single, insidious program can destroy data, and even hard drives, before you can do anything. With a home network, that virus can move from one PC in your home to the next.

Many people avoid antivirus software because it is too time consuming. But when there are multiple networked PCs in the home, it doesn't have to be. The accompanying CD includes a network version of VirusNet, which enables you to automate the entire antivirus process.

Viruses can come into your network in a number of ways:

- In a downloaded file
- On a diskette received from a friend or colleague, who may not check for viruses
- In an attachment to an e-mail
- From a Web page in the form of a Java or ActiveX component

There have even been reports of viruses found on commercial software.

VirusNet prevents a range of viruses, including those found in word-processing macros and even Java. Here's how to set up the product:

1. Install the program with the user interface on the CD accompanying this book, or install manually by double-clicking the file vnlan 300.exe in the directory \Get Network to Work for You\VirusNet\ on the CD.

2. Click Start, then Programs, and VirusNet LAN.

3. Click the help file for directions on how to use VirusNet.

Set Up a De-Virusized Zone

Even though you probably need antivirus software for each computer, it is wise to create a directory for files from the outside. All files, whether downloaded or copied from a diskette, should go into this directory. Using virus-scanning software, examine the files for any problems.

You can use a download directory with your e-mail system, too. Go into the e-mail program's configuration tools and specify the download directory as the location for any attachments. Then all you need to do is check files as they go into the directory.

Regularly Update Antivirus Protection

Most antivirus programs keep information on existing viruses for the purpose of scanning files. Such lists go out of date quickly because of the prolific nature of those who write viruses. For that reason, you need to update the virus products often. With a registered version of VirusLAN, you can update all the antivirus software on the network at the same time:

1. Using a browser, go to www.safetynet.com.

2. Download vnupdate.exe.

3. Copy the file to C:\VNWIN, or whatever directory you specified during the product's installation.

4. Go to the LAN Management Console, and click Deploy Update.

15 Troubleshoot Network Problems

Nothing is perfect in this life, especially networks. There are many things that can go wrong, from small and annoying hardware errors to misconfigurations of software as well as the major breakdowns of all order that seem part and parcel with the use of computers.

When you have problems—and you will—it's important to know how to solve them. More important than a checklist of symptoms and possible causes, such as a car-repair manual, you need to concentrate on the right approach. The general steps are

♦ Note what you know.

♦ Isolate the problem.

♦ Use diagnostic tools.

♦ Check the cables.

While you can't predict potential problems, taking a methodical and planned approach will help solve them.

Note What You Know

Can you imagine playing poker and using only four of your five cards? It would be almost impossible to win. An equivalent event often happens when people face technical problems. Caught up by a problem, they forget all the information they actually have. Here are some practices that may help:

♦ Take a pad of paper and write down everything you can see about the problem. Don't dismiss the smallest piece of information.

♦ An error dialog box may offer a number or text that will assist you in finding help in a product reference book. The error message might even indicate which program is having the problem.

- ◆ Select Settings ➢ Control Panel ➢ System. Click Device Manager, and look for any yellow exclamation points. They indicate a problem with hardware and provide an error message that can be helpful.

- ◆ Make a list of any new hardware or software you may have installed into the machines having problems. If you added something, take it out, and see whether that improves the situation.

Having all the information at hand may provide you with a sudden insight or clue to the cure for your network's difficulty.

Isolate the Problem

Like a car, what often makes network problems difficult to diagnose is the number of interconnected elements involved. Aside from a phone number of an on-call expert, the best tool you can have is the habit of isolating a problem. Look at the problem and consider its potential causes. Then you know to focus your investigation on those causes and not other issues. Take your list of information, and see what you can rule in or out.

For instance, say that one computer on a peer-to-peer network won't connect with the others, but the computer works fine on its own. Logically there follows three possible causes:

- ◆ All the other computers are incorrectly configured and won't recognize the one PC.

- ◆ The one PC is incorrectly configured and won't recognize the other PCs.

- ◆ There is something wrong with either the cables or connectors.

You can now investigate each area more methodically to find the actual cause of the problem. Sometimes the nature of the problem itself offers important information. Say you have set up a network; you go to one of your computers, start a word processor, and open a file on another PC. So far, so good. You make some changes, but suddenly find you can't save the file on the remote location. Because the file opens but you can't save a modification, it is a good chance that the problem is on the remote system—either there is a problem with the drive or you have read-only permission to that directory.

Use Diagnostic Tools

Any mechanic has tools that can measure electrical output and resistance, compression in the engine, and tire pressure. If you are reading this section, you are probably the system administrator of your castle, if not the ruling monarch. To save your time and find problems faster, use the diagnostic tools that some benign programmer left for you.

Both Windows NT and NetWare have sophisticated tools to measure performance of your network. A peer-to-peer system may or may not come with such tools. Windows peer-to-peer networks, though, have a number of tools, which are covered in "16. Check TCP/IP Performance with Ping and Winipcfg."

Check the Cables

Cables and connectors can cause many network problems and should be the first item to check if a machine cannot connect to the network. You can separate this into three distinct areas:

- ◆ Cables that connect a computer to a jack
- ◆ Cables that run inside the walls
- ◆ Patch panels

Cables running from a computer to a wall jack often cause problems. Possible problems include wires that have worked loose from a connector after being pulled, or connectors that aren't crimped tightly enough, or flaws in the cable itself.

In any case, take a known good cable, such as one that is working on another computer, and use it to replace the one with a suspected fault. If the problematic PC seems cured, then the cable is bad. See whether either of the connectors seems loose or damaged. If so, replace it, and see whether the cable now works.

It is possible that a cable in the wall is a problem. This can happen if the cable is not well connected to the inside of the jack, or it might mean that you bent the cable too sharply (more than 90 degrees) somewhere in its run. You can get test equipment that will inject a sound signal over two wires in the cable. By listening on the other end, you can literally hear whether the wires are providing a solid connection.

A cheaper way of doing this is to use a transistor radio. Open it, and disconnect the wires to the speaker. Attach the speaker wires to two of the cable wires at one end. Bring the speaker to the other end and connect the far ends of the wires to the speakers. You should be able to hear the signal. By methodically testing pairs of wires, you can see whether all the wires are good. If so, the problem is elsewhere. If not, prepare to pull more cable.

The final place to check is the patch panel. It's very easy to make a mistake and connect an unused cable to the hub, accidentally overlooking the cable that is actually connected to the computer in question. This is a good place to check if you are running the network for the first time or if you have just moved a device from one jack to another.

16   Check TCP/IP Performance with Ping and Winipcfg

Windows 98 comes with many tools that help you understand the state of your network if you use TCP/IP as the networking protocol. Two of the best tools to use are Ping and Winipcfg.

Use Ping to Diagnose Network Problems

One of the basic tools in diagnosing a network is a ping utility. You send a message, called a *ping,* from one point on the network to another device on the network. The far end receives the ping and then immediately turns around and resends the ping to you. Your computer then displays the amount of time the round-trip took.

If ping can't find a particular computer, try ping from some other PCs on the network. Through trial and error, you can quickly find out whether the problem is isolated between a pair of computers or whether one of the PCs is off the network.

When a ping returns with a time, you have a relative reference for how well the network is operating. Typical values will depend on the type of network you are running, both the physical connections used to carry signals as well as the NOS. It is a good practice to use ping from time to time, especially early on, to get a feel for what is normal for your network. Then you will know when performance is significantly off.

Using ping is actually easy, though it doesn't have a graphical user interface. On a Windows machine, no matter what version, do the following:

1. Open a DOS session.

2. Type the command **c: ping [name]**, where *[name]* is the computer name for the computer you want to receive the ping.

3. Read the results.

Be sure to close the DOS box after you are done with ping. Ping also accepts the Internet address of the computer. If the computer name does not work, try the Internet address of the computer. To determine the Internet address of the computer, use Winipcfg, which is discussed next.

Use Winipcfg to Diagnose Network Problems

You won't find winipcfg anywhere on the Start menu, but it is handy. It gives you a range of information about the host and your PC's NIC. Follow these steps to use the program:

1. Click Start.

2. Select Run.

3. Type **winipcfg**, and click OK.

What you will see is a window with extensive information on the IP (Internet) address of your computer and server names, which is important for tracking down TCP/IP problems. Be sure to click the More Info button to get the full screen, shown below.

17   **Stay Legal**

When you install software, there is always a licensing agreement, which spells out what rights you have to the software and under what conditions you may use it. Unlike most products, you don't buy software, but you actually license it. That means you pay the company that makes the software for the right to use it.

Recently, there have been stories in the news about individuals and companies being prosecuted for illegally using software. The best way to escape prosecution is to avoid grounds for it. That license agreement—which, if you are like most people, you don't read—is the way to bypass legal hassles.

Different vendors offer different types of licensing. Some will only allow you to install software on one computer at a time. If you want to put a copy on a second computer, you must remove it from the first. Other companies, aware of the prevalence of people using more than one computer to get things done, will let you install a product on multiple computers, so long as you use it on one at a time only. Still others will allow other members of your household to use the software, but only if no one else is using it at the same time.

Before loading applications onto a network, be sure you are doing so legally. If you are not allowed to have the software on more than one computer at the same time, you could still probably put it on one machine and run it over the network. (See "11. Share Applications across the Network.") If it is a program that would require being installed on every computer to properly run over the network, you are out of luck.

18 Maintain Hard-Drive Performance

Your whole network only works as well as its hard drives do. By taking a little time, you can keep hard drives in top shape and keep an eye out for potential problems. Here are a few of the benefits you will see:

◆ Systems work faster.

◆ The network runs faster.

◆ You can catch hard-drive problems before you lose data.

You can split your time between defragmenting the hard drive to keep it performing well and using SMARTmonitor to catch problems before they occur.

Defragment Your Drive for Speed

In the normal course of operation, a computer writes data all over a hard drive. In the process, the operating system splits many files into pieces that can be scattered over the hard drive. When this happens, it takes longer to read and modify files.

Defragmentation programs analyze the hard drive and rearrange the blocks of data so that related blocks are next to each other. Windows 95, 98, and NT all have defragmentation utilities built-in.

Because it must rearrange all the bits of files, the defragmentation program should have sole access to the hard drive. It follows that it's best to run defragmentation when you have nothing else to do, such as in the middle of the night. Once a week should be often enough for defragmenting. Here's how to do it.

1. Click Start ➢ Accessories ➢ System Tools.

2. Select Disk Defragmenter.

3. Choose the drive you want to defragment, and then click OK.

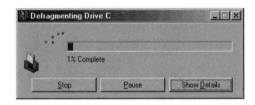

Depending on the size of the hard drive, defragmentation can take a good hour or more. To run it in the middle of the night, use Scheduled Tasks.

1. Click Start ➢ Accessories ➢ System Tools.

2. Select Scheduled Tasks.

3. Double-click Add Scheduled Task, which starts the wizard.

4. Click Next, and then scroll through the list of programs until you find Scheduled Tasks.

5. Select Disk Defragmenter, and click Next.

6. Choose the frequency for the task, and click Next.

7. Fill in the time and day to run the job.

8. Click Next, and then Finish.

Now you will be able to defragment your drive without loosing valuable time—or sleep.

Keep Problems in Check with SMARTmonitor

Hard drives keep precisely aligned, extremely flat platters spinning at ridiculously high speeds while metal arms slide in and out between them. This is equipment designed for eventual disaster. SMARTmonitor from

SystemSoft is a program that keeps tabs on how well your hard drives are running. It works with S.M.A.R.T. (Self-Monitoring Analysis and Reporting Technology) drives, which can monitor their own performance. Virtually all new hard drives are S.M.A.R.T.-compliant.

The program monitors all the drives on your network periodically and warns you when a drive is close to failing, permitting you to save your data before you lose it. To install it, copy the SMARTmonitor file from the CD to your hard drive. Start Windows Explorer, highlight the file, and double-click it. It will install itself.

Here's how to use it:

1. Open Start ➤ Settings ➤ Control Panel ➤ SMARTmonitor.

2. Select the Disks tab. It displays the drive letters and whether the drives are S.M.A.R.T.

3. Select the Settings tab. Be sure to check the Always Run SMARTmonitor when Stating Windows and Display SMARTmonitor disk icons in the system tray.

4. Click the Start SMARTmonitor button.

5. If any of the drives have monitoring turned off, then the Monitor All Disk Drives button is active. Press it.

6. Click OK.

7. To check on drive status, right-click the SMARTmonitor icon, and choose Status Check.

In case of an imminent disk failure, SMARTmonitor will display a warning. If you see it, back up the data from that drive as quickly as you can.

Survive a Hard-Drive Crash

There may be times that despite care, a hard-drive crashes. Hopefully, you have a backup. Even if you do, there may be cases where you can't use the backup, such as being away from home with a laptop that has hard-drive problems or if the machine with problems is also the one connected to the tape drive. In those circumstances, there are still steps you can take.

1. Move the tape drive to another machine and install the backup software. You can then replace the defective hard drive if necessary and run the restore part of the backup software.

2. Buy a new hard drive if necessary. If not, format a hard drive with the appropriate operating system, install it, and then reinstall the tape-drive software. You can now run the restore part of the backup software.

3. Use a data-recovery service. Some companies recover data from hard drives that have crashed or have had other problems.

But if you've been backing up the network regularly, the most data you will lose will be one day's worth.

19 Let Computers Talk with a Network Protocol

You wouldn't operate an automobile without knowing the rules of the road—at least, so your fellow motorists hope. Networks also have rules of the road called *protocols*. Unlike driving, there are different sets of rules for networks. One use of your network, such as connecting to the Internet, might require TCP/IP, whereas another, such as sharing files in a Windows network, might be better served by NetBUEI.

Fortunately, you can run multiple protocols at the same time if you need to. Adding a protocol is easy under Windows. Just follow these steps:

1. Right-click Network Neighborhood on the desktop.

2. Select Properties.

3. Click the Configuration tab. You can scroll through the window to see whether the protocol you want is there. In the screen shot below, for example, TCP/IP is there but not NetBUEI.

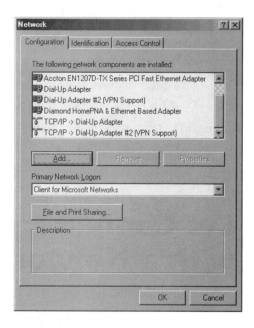

4. To add NetBUEI, click the Add button. **Highlight the Protocol entry,** and click Add **again.**

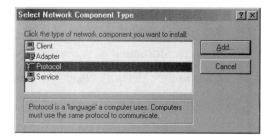

5. Highlight the manufacturer, in this case Microsoft, and the protocol, and click OK. The protocol is now on the list under the Configuration tab. When the protocol loads, the computer may request the Operating System disk. Insert the disk in the CD-ROM, and click OK.

Besides adding protocols, you can also add clients for particular types of networks as well as adapters, though NICs usually add the latter automatically.

Connect to Your Home Network on the Run

Home networks are wonderfully convenient, but they can't do much good when their owners can't use them. Connect a portable computer to the network and you open new realms of usefulness. Here are just a few of the dozens of reasons you might want to connect your portable to your network, whether at home or from a distance:

◆ Update organizers so you always have the latest information, whether on a desktop or handheld organizer.

◆ Keep task lists with you.

◆ Move files from the network to a portable and back again.

◆ Use networked CD and DVD drives from a portable.

◆ Print documents from a portable.

◆ Use a handheld as a note-taking station at a telephone.

◆ Retrieve important files when you're away from home.

This part of the book explains how to connect portable computers to your network and how to get access to your network and e-mail when away from home.

20 Connect Handheld Devices to Your Home Network

Their light weight and small size make handheld computers practical electronic personal-information managers. By keeping the information synchronized on both a desktop and a handheld, you avoid the danger of keeping two different schedules or contact lists and forgetting which is up-to-date. (See "26. Synchronize Data between Your Portable and Your Network.")

Before you can synchronize a handheld with a desktop, you need to connect them. Depending on the type of handheld computer you have—a Palm from 3Com or a Windows CE device from a number of vendors, including Compaq, NEC, and Casio—you can connect directly to the PC, or you might have the option of connecting to the network.

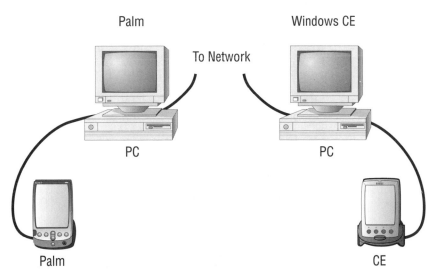

Connect a Handheld Device to a Networked PC

Either a Palm or Windows CE computer can connect directly to a PC on your network, giving the handhelds access to the network through the PC. The advantage of a direct connection is that you can synchronize organizing data between the handheld and the network through the desktop.

The Palm IIIx, for example, sits in a cradle that connects to a networked PC easily. To connect the Palm to a PC, do the following steps:

1. Connect the cable from the Palm's cradle to the serial port of the desktop computer.

2. Insert the Palm into the cradle.

3. Install the necessary software to connect to your desktop organizing software. (See "26. Synchronize Data between Your Portable and Your Network.")

When you aren't using the Palm, you can leave it in the cradle without a problem.

Although Windows CE devices differ, they can typically connect to a networked PC in two ways: through a serial cable or via a wireless infrared link. Because few PCs have infrared hardware, it makes more sense to concentrate on the serial connections. You use a special cable that comes with the device because most CE computers have nonstandard serial connectors. The following is a typical scenario:

1. Install the Windows CE desktop software on your Windows PC.

2. Connect the nonstandard end of the serial cable to the handheld.

3. Connect the standard serial connector of the cable to one of the PC's serial ports.

4. Double-click on the Mobile Devices icon on the desktop.

5. If you haven't enabled serial communications for Mobile Devices yet, go to the Files menu, and choose Communications. Click the Enabled checkbox under Device Connections via Serial Port. Choose the correct port number, and then click OK.

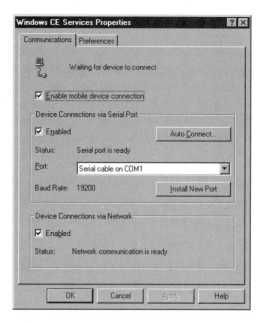

One consideration for at least the 2.1.1 version of Windows CE is that it only supports serial speeds of 19,200 baud, which is considerably slower than many other examples of serial communications. You may have to configure both machines to the right value for the serial line to work.

The following steps configure a Windows 98 PC serial port to work with the CE handheld:

1. Click Start ➤ Settings ➤ Control Panel.

2. Double-click System.

3. Click the Device Manager tab.

4. Click the plus sign next to Ports.

5. Highlight the port you want to use, and then click the Properties button.

6. Click the Port Settings tab.

7. Choose 19200 in the Bits per Second box.

8. Click OK twice, and then close the Control Panel.

9. Close all programs, and then reboot the system so the values can take effect.

Now the PC is ready to communicate with the Windows CE handheld.

Now you have to configure the Windows CE serial port to run at 19,200 baud:

1. Click on Start ➤ Settings ➤ Control Panel.

2. Double-click on Communications Properties.

3. Click the PC Communications tab.

4. If the value showing is not 19200, click the Change button.

5. Pick Serial Port @ 19200, click OK twice, and close the Control Panel.

You are now set to have your handheld and desktop work together.

Connect a Handheld Device Directly to Your Network

The other way of connecting a handheld to a PC is through your network. In the case of the Palm, that means connecting through a PC on the network or using a modem to call a PC. A Windows CE device can either use a modem to call a PC or connect directly to the network.

Connect a Palm Device to Your Home Network

With a Palm handheld, you have two choices. One is to hook the Palm to the serial port of any PC on the network, and then connect over the network to synchronize with a particular PC. This makes sense if the target PC with the information already uses its serial ports for other uses, such as a modem and mouse, and cannot dedicate one to the Palm. The other way is to connect to the network through a dial-up server using the optional Palm Modem. (See "22. Remotely Access Your Home Network with a Windows 98 Dial-Up Server.")

NOTE To access the network through a dial-up server, the network must run TCP/IP, which may mean adding software called *TCP/IP adapters* to computers on the network. (See "19. Let Computers Talk with a Network Protocol.")

NOTE If you are connecting the cradle to another PC on the network, both PCs must have the Palm Desktop software installed.

Before you can connect the Palm and PC over the network for the first time, you must connect the Palm cradle to the serial port on the PC that will synchronize with the handheld. This procedure will set up the transfer of needed network information to the handheld:

1. Click the HotSync icon in the Windows system tray.

2. Click on Network and then Setup.

3. Select the Network tab, and put a checkbox next to your name. Then click OK.

4. Put the Palm in its cradle, and press the HotSync button.

5. After the HotSync function is done, remove the Palm from its cradle, turn it on, and tap the Applications icon.

6. Tap the HotSync icon and then the Menu icon.

7. Select Options and then Modem Sync Prefs.

8. Tap Network and then OK.

Now when you connect the Palm through the network, it will synchronize with this PC.

If you want to connect a Palm to the network through a phone call, set up the Palm Modem as follows:

1. Start the HotSync Manager.

2. Select the Modem tab, and then set the Serial Port to the correct port. You can get this number by clicking Start ➢ Control Panel; double-click Modem, and check the port number for your modem.

3. Set Speed to As Fast As Possible. If you have problems having the two communicate, you can adjust this downward.

4. Set the modem to the proper type. If unsure, select Hayes Basic.

5. If the modem manufacturer suggests a setup string, enter it in the Setup String window.

6. Click OK, and then turn on the Palm

7. Select Applications and then HotSync.

8. Tap Enter Phone #, and then enter the appropriate information. Click OK.

9. Select Menu ➢ Options ➢ Modem Setup. Enter the information about the modem and phone you will use.

You are now set to synchronize the Palm and the networked PC over the network.

Connect a CE Handheld Directly to Your Home Network

CE devices come with a slot for PC Cards (previously known as PCMCIA). That means you can *directly* connect the handheld to the network without an intermediary by using an NE2000-compatible Ethernet PC Card. Not only does this let you escape from dedicating a serial port to the device but opens new avenues of use throughout the house, such as message-taking stations at phones.

To connect the handheld to your network, insert the Ethernet PC Card in the slot on the side of the device. When you insert the card into the handheld, you will see the NE2000 Compatible Ethernet Driver Settings dialog box.

1. Although the product's directions probably tell you to select "Obtain an IP Address via DHCP," choose to set an address manually, because you probably are not running a DHCP server. IP addresses are sets of four numbers, called *octets*, each of which can range from 0 to 255. You could, for example, pick 200.200.200.1. The first octet cannot be greater than 223. The second and third octet cannot be greater than 255. The last octet cannot be greater than 254.

NOTE If you are using a proxy server (see "37. Share Your Internet Connection over the Network"), for security reasons, you want to use an address that can't be passed over the Internet. To ensure this, pick an address of the form 10.0.0.x, where x can range from 1 to 254. Proxy servers don't pass these addresses over the Internet, and you have over 250 available addresses, which should be plenty. Be sure not to use the same address twice.

2. Choose Start ➤ Settings ➤ Control Panel.

3. Double-click or tap the Network icon.

4. Click on the Adapters tab, and then select NE2000 Compatible Ethernet Driver.

5. Select the Identification tab, and type in the username and password you want to use to log in.

6. Go to your PC and double-click the Mobile Devices icon. Select File from the menu. Be sure Enable Network Connection is checked. If not, click it once. Then click Close.

The network should use the NetBEUI protocol. (See "19. Let Computers Talk with a Network Protocol.") On the PC, you must also configure for a network connection.

1. Double-click the Mobile Devices icon on the desktop.

2. Click File, and then click Enable Network Connection.

3. Click Close.

When you connect the CE device to the network, you will see the Connection screen. Select Network Connection, and you will have access to the network.

You can also dial into the network. After following the directions for a direct network connection, be sure that you have an account on the dial-up server. (See "22. Remotely Access Your Home Network with a Windows 98 Dial-Up Server.") Next, create a connection on the CE device as follows:

1. Click Start ➤ Programs ➤ Communication ➤ Remote Networking.

2. Double-click the Make New Connection icon.

3. Enter a name for the connection, select Dial-Up Connection, and then click Next.

4. Select a modem (if you have a choice), and click Configure. Enter the connection settings, and then click OK.

5. Click Next and enter the phone number and dialing information. Click Finish.

When you want to dial in, click Start ➤ Programs ➤ Communication ➤ Remote Networking. Double-click your connection icon and the system will dial your server.

21 Connect Your Notebook or Laptop to Your Home Network

Not only does a laptop or notebook give you the full power of a computer when you're away from the home or office but you can get complete access to your network from anywhere. Forget a file? It's as near as a phone call. Want to use a DVD drive with an older laptop? Hook into your network and you're ready to go. You can also keep versions of files that are on your portable organized and synchronized. If you work at home, you can keep everything on a portable. That way, you have all your business files where you need them, but you can back them up easily to the network to avoid disaster and even use your home printer without moving a cable.

You have a couple of options for hooking up your laptop or notebook computer to your home network. These include accessing network resources by connecting the portable computer to a networked desktop device and by connecting the portable computer directly to the network. Although the latter is easier, it also requires that you have a network adapter for your laptop, which can set you back several hundred dollars.

Connect a Laptop to a PC to Access Network Resources

If you have a small home network without a spare port on your hub for a laptop, you can still access many network resources from your portable computer by connecting it directly to a desktop computer on the network. You can connect the two machines with a special *null-modem* cable, which will allow you to access files on other parts of the network. The cable is designed to run between the serial ports or the parallel ports of the two machines.

NOTE Running a cable between the parallel ports provides faster access than using the serial ports and is certainly cheaper than a NIC.

Windows 98 has built-in support, called a Direct Cable Connection, for this type of transfer. You can move files between the two machines or, because the desktop is connected to your network, between the portable and any network location. To use a Direct Cable Connection, have your computers run the NetBEUI protocol. (See "19. Let Computers Talk with a Network Protocol.") One restriction is that you can't use Direct Cable Connection at the same time as Dial-Up Networking, because the two use a common file that can't do double duty.

You have to install Direct Cable Connection on each of the two computers that you will connect with the cable. To do this, follow these steps on both your laptop or notebook and the networked computer to which you want to connect:

1. Click Start ➢ Control Panel.

2. Double-click Add/Remove Programs.

3. Click the Windows Setup tab.

4. Click Communications in the Components list, and then select Details.

5. Select Direct Cable Connection in the Components dialog box, and then click OK.

Now both your portable computer and your networked PC should be ready to use the Direct Cable Connection.

To actually use a Direct Cable Connection, use this procedure:

1. Connect the transfer cable to both computers.

2. On the portable, click Start ➤ Programs ➤ Accessories ➤ Communications. Choose Direct Cable Connection.

The first time you run Direct Cable Connection, the system will start a wizard that will help you configure the connection.

Connect a Portable Computer Directly to the Network

Because laptops and notebooks run Windows 95 and 98, they have an easy time connecting to home networks. They also can take better advantage of network resources than handhelds, including

◆ Printers

◆ CD-ROM and DVD-ROM drives

◆ Fax servers

◆ Applications

◆ Shared high-speed Internet access

To connect the portable to your home network, you need a NIC. If the computer supports PC Cards, you can get an Ethernet PC Card. If the portable is an older model, you may be stuck with a parallel port NIC. There are also some that support both 10/100baseT and HomePNA networking, so you can connect to an Ethernet network at work and a phone line network at home. In any case, the connection will be much faster than a NIC that connects to a parallel port.

With these steps, connecting the portable computer to the network is easy:

1. Insert the PC Card, and install the accompanying software according to the vendor's instructions.

2. Configure your system with the correct workgroup and computer names to work with Windows peer-to-peer networking. If you are using another network operating system, install the proper client software. (See "9. Set Up the Network Software.")

3. Connect a cable between the portable and an RJ-45 wall jack.

Your portable is now part of the network, just like any desktop PC in your home.

22 Remotely Access Your Home Network with a Windows 98 Dial-Up Server

There are many reasons why you might want to dial in to your home network from the road, ranging from checking your grocery list to grabbing a copy of a program file that you accidentally erased.

To set up a dial-up server, you need the following:

◆ A computer designated as the server

◆ A modem attached to that server

◆ A correctly configured network operating system.

A dial-up connection requires two components: a client, which is the computer that is dialing in, and a server, which accepts the call and provides network access. Fortunately, Windows 98 peer-to-peer networking includes the ability to do this. There are a few caveats that you should be aware of:

◆ You can connect only one modem to a Windows dial-up server, so only one person can call in at a time.

◆ Both the dial-up server and client must run the same protocol. You should choose NetBEUI, so that the client can have full access to the rest of the network.

◆ The Windows 98 server cannot host a virtual private network, which is a way of creating a private network over the Internet.

Even with those restrictions, the ease of setting up the server, as well as the low cost of Windows 98, makes it a good choice for a home network.

NOTE You can also create a dial-up server using Windows NT Server or Novell NetWare network operating systems. To find out how to accomplish this task, please refer to *Mastering Windows NT Server 4,* by Mark Minasi (Sybex, 1999) or *Mastering NetWare 5,* by James Gaskin (Sybex, 1999).

Install the Windows 98 Dial-Up Server

Becuase Windows 98 doesn't automatically install the Dial-Up Server software, you will need to add it to your system. You can do so as follows:

1. Click on Start ➢ Settings ➢ Control Panel.

2. Double-click Add/Remove Programs, and select the Windows Setup tab.

3. Double-click Communications.

4. Check Dial-Up Server. Click OK twice.

Now you can physically call into your network. But there are a couple more steps before you start dialing.

Set Dial-Up Security under Windows 98

Having a dial-up server potentially leaves your network open to anyone who gets the phone number of the modem. While you could assume that no one would be interested in using your network, you should consider your choices for security on a Windows 98 Dial-Up server:

No security   Even for a home network this is a foolish choice. You will have schedules, financial information, control of a home security system, access to your Internet account, and other items of value on your network.

Share-level security   Under share-level security, you set a single password for the Dial-Up server. Anyone with the password can dial into your network. You can limit the access of a dial-up user to particular files or directories, but because you are probably going to dial-in, you may be reluctant to overly restrict yourself.

User-level security   You can create user profiles with different passwords and degrees of access. To use this option, you need a computer on your network running either Windows NT Server or NetWare.

Of the three choices, the second is the best for most home networks by default. You will want some security, but you are probably not running a client/server NOS. Here is how to set share-level security:

1. Be sure File and Printer Sharing services are installed. (See "19. Let Computers Talk with a Network Protocol.")

2. Click Start ➤ Accessories ➤ Communications ➤ Dial-Up Networking.

3. Choose the Connections menu, and then select Dial-Up Server.

4. Click Allow Caller Access, and then click Change Password. Click OK.

Now that you have set up the server and configured the dial-up security, all that is left is to prepare the portable as a dial-up client.

NOTE   Security isn't much help if anyone can guess your password. Don't choose something that would be easy to guess, such as your own name or birth date. A meaningless combination of letters and numbers make sneaking into your network much harder. You might also consider changing the password every few weeks.

Get Clients Ready to Dial-Up

You have to configure the clients as well as the server to use Dial-Up Networking. Be sure that Dial-Up Networking (DUN) is installed on each client device that may be used to remotely access your network. This may include any laptops and notebooks, a desktop computer at your office (if a firewall does not prevent it), and home computers of friends and family.

If Dial-Up Networking is not installed, here's how to add it:

1. Click Start ➢ Settings ➢ Control Panel.

2. Double-click Add/Remove Programs.

3. Select the Windows Setup tab, and double-click Communications.

4. Select Dial-Up Networking, click OK, and then click Apply.

The client needs a modem. If it doesn't have one, purchase a modem and install it according to the vendor's instructions. Next, create a dial-up connection for your home network.

1. Choose Start ➢ Accessories ➢ Communications ➢ Dial-Up Networking.

2. Double-click Make New Connection.

3. Devise a name for the connection, such as PC Phone Home.

4. Select the modem to use, and then click Next.

5. Type in the phone number that the dial-up server's modem uses.

6. Click Finish.

Your portable is now ready to dial into your home network at the double-click of a mouse with the following steps:

1. Be sure your dial-up server and modem are on and that the modem is connected to the proper phone line.

2. From the remote location, connect a phone cable from the portable to a telephone line.

3. Open Dial-Up Networking, and double-click the connection.

Your software should take care of the rest of the details. You can now freely use network resources from wherever you are.

23 Use LapLink Professional to Connect a Portable Computer to a Networked Computer

A slick and powerful solution to connecting a portable to your home network is LapLink Professional from Traveling Software. Over the years, this product has grown from a file-transfer utility to a sophisticated remote access and control package. You have several choices of how you can connect:

◆ Connect the portable directly to a PC on the network. You can do it with a special serial cable, a parallel cable, or even a USB cable.

◆ If the portable is connected directly to the network, you can use LapLink over the network.

◆ You can use dial-up networking and run LapLink over the phone connection.

Because LapLink gives you tremendous flexibility in deciding which files you will transfer from one computer to the next, and in automating the process, it is a better choice than trying to copy files by hand through Windows Explorer.

Not only can you swap files but you can remotely control the desktop from the portable and use printers anywhere on the network. A Direct Cable Connection restricts itself to providing file access.

To connect the two computers, install LapLink on both of them. Connect the transfer cable between them and follow the vendor's directions for transferring the files.

NOTE If you plan to transfer files between the portable and a networked hard drive, be sure that you have the necessary file and directory access.

24 Access Your Home Network via the Internet

You could use a dial-up server and phone into your network, but that might mean long-distance phone charges. Why not use the Internet for your connection? That means anywhere you could get onto the Internet, you could reach your home network.

If you have gone the client/server route, you could consider creating a *virtual private network*, or VPN, that generates a private network running through the Internet. Unfortunately, this can be pretty complex. Refer to *Mastering Network Security*, by Chris Brenton (Sybex, 1999), for more information.

A much easier approach is to use Microsoft Personal Web Server (PWS) with Windows 98 and then give yourself access to all files through an Internet connection. This lets you run an actual Web server and connect it to the Internet. In the section "40. Create Your Own Web Server," it explains how to install and configure PWS. PWS can't handle more than a few people using it at one time, but if your intent is to provide remote access for your household and maybe a few close friends, that shouldn't be a problem. There are a few considerations:

◆ Your Web server has to be running when you need access. Either someone in your home must connect it at those times or you need a continuous Internet connection, such as DSL or cable.

◆ You will want password security so anyone stumbling across your Web site won't have unfettered access to your network. PWS documentation has instructions on how to add password support to PWS through Active Server Page *scripts* and instructions for the Web server.

◆ PWS will not publish a network drive's contents, so you can access only what is on the local hard drives of the computer hosting PWS. To get around the problem, run PWS from your file server.

◆ You will need a connection to an ISP from wherever you are to reach your Web server.

While your Web server is running, log into an ISP, and start a browser. Enter the URL that you have from setting up the PWS. You will now come to your Web server's home page. Provide your name and password, and you can have access to your file server.

....

N O T E   Microsoft Personal Web Server is on your Windows 98 installation CD.

25   Get Your E-mail while on the Road

One of the main reasons you might want remote access to your network is to check your e-mail. Conveniently, you can do this in many ways, from dialing in to your network to having your e-mail follow you.

Use Remote Access to Get Your E-mail

If you have a Dial-Up Server for your network (see "22. Remotely Access Your Home Network with a Windows 98 Dial-Up Server"), you can dial-in for your e-mail. The trick is to have your e-mail client software get your e-mail for you. You can instruct software such as Eudora and Microsoft Outlook to get your e-mail on a regular basis.

The way you would do this with Microsoft Outlook Express is as follows:

1. From the Tools menu, pick Options.

2. Select the General tab.

3. Be sure there is a check mark next to "Check for New Messages Every," and choose the number of minutes between checks. You can specify any number of minutes, up to 999, between e-mail checks. If you want to check your e-mail four times a day, have the program check four times a day, or every 360 minutes. To be able to check every hour, set the time to 60.

4. Select the Dial Up tab and be sure there are checks next to Automatically Dial when Checking for New Messages and Hang Up when Finished Sending, Receiving, or Downloading. Click OK.

5. Now select Accounts from the Tools menu.

6. Select the Mail tab, and highlight your e-mail account; then click on Properties.

7. Select the Connection tab.

8. If Outlook Express is using a modem on the PC running it, then check Connect Using My Phone Line, and select the right connection from the list. If, on the other hand, Outlook Express will use a networked Internet connection (see "37. Share Your Internet Connection over the Network"), then click Connect Using My Local Area Network (LAN).

By configuring Outlook Express this way, you ensure that it will dial out to request e-mail on a regular basis and then hang up the phone after each session with the mail server is over.

If the e-mail client has to dial up an ISP, there are two steps you need to take. One is to configure the package to hang up the phone line after it sends and receives e-mail. Check the vendor's directions on how to set this. The other step, since you are probably using the Microsoft phone dialer, is to check the box that enables auto-dialing, as the image below shows.

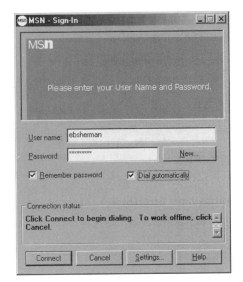

To get your mail when away from home, dial-up the network and synchronize your portable with your desktop, which will include your e-mail. Then read your e-mail, reply as necessary, dial a second time, and resynchronize so your outgoing mail is now in your desktop mail client. The next time the software checks with the mail server you use, it will send your messages.

Have Your E-mail Follow You

You can have your e-mail follow you to another account where you can pick it up. That second account can be a Web-based free e-mail system, such as Hotmail (www.hotmail.com), or some other account, such as your e-mail account at work.

Some ISPs or e-mail servers will offer this capability of *redirecting* e-mails. Check with your e-mail service provider for more information. If such a service is not available, you can still effectively redirect your e-mail by forwarding the messages to the appropriate account. Major e-mail packages, such as Microsoft Outlook and Eudora, have tools to create rules for automatically handling e-mail. Besides moving the e-mail to particular folders, you can also create a rule to forward all e-mail.

Next, configure the e-mail client to get mail on a regular basis according to the vendor's instructions. If the e-mail software has to call an ISP, have the software hang up the phone after sending and receiving mail. As you did for remote access to e-mail earlier in this section, set the phone dialer to auto-dial.

All you have to do to get your mail is to check the e-mail account to which you forwarded the e-mail.

WARNING Replying to e-mails will require some thought if you have forwarded the message to yourself, because the return address will be your own. Be sure to check the e-mail for the address that originally sent the message to you. Manually insert that address into the recipient field of your return message. Now you can send the e-mail.

Three Ways to Have a Computer Read Your E-mail Aloud

It may sound like something out of a science-fiction television series, but with the current capabilities of voice synthesis, a computer can actually read your e-mail to you using software, such as Conversa Messenger from Conversational Computing or Mercury Mobile from CenturionSoft.

Conversa Messenger can take your phone call and read the contents of your e-mail over the phone. It also handles voice mail and faxes and offers many other features.

Mercury Mobile handles just e-mail, not the range of communications that Conversa Messenger can manage. However, Mercury Mobile can also telephone a number you give it, such as a cell phone, and read your e-mail to you. Combine that with voice-mail for the phone, and you know you will get your messages.

There is also a free e-mail service called Shoutmail.com. You can call it from a telephone, and the server will read your e-mail to you. It will even record a voice response to the e-mail. The server returns a note to the sender, telling the person to check a particular site on the Web to hear your answer. You can find the service at www.shoutmail.com.

Send E-mail to Your Pager

If you can't wait to get your e-mail, consider a paging service that can send your e-mail to you. Such companies provide an e-mail address for you to use. Any e-mail the service receives is turned into an alphanumeric message and sent to your pager.

You don't have to have all your e-mail go to this address. Instead, use the directions earlier in this section for redirecting or forwarding your e-mail. Then, when you have regular access to your e-mail again, stop sending the e-mail on to the pager.

NOTE An example is the Motorola PageWriter 2000X using the SkyTel paging service. You can both send and receive e-mail from this pager as well as get both numeric and text pages.

26 Synchronize Data between Your Portable and Your Network

A problem with using mobile computers is that you often need the same information on both the portable and a desktop. That can be a problem when you change something like a phone number or presentation on one computer and want to ensure that you have the same information on another.

That's when synchronizing data comes in handy. Software tracks different versions of files and information and makes sure that the most current version is the one that appears on both the network and the portable.

WARNING Synchronizing software is helpful, not omniscient. If you make two sets of independent changes on two different machines, you run the risk of the software assuming that the last changes you made were the only ones. The software will copy the later version over the earlier one, and you will lose one set of changes. Be sure to synchronize after you make changes on any machine.

Synchronize Your Handheld

Since Palm organizers and Windows CE devices are designed around synchronizing data, they come with special synchronization software. When you connect the handheld to your PC, either directly, via dial-up, or over the network, the software can automatically update the information on both sides. This includes moving files back and forth as necessary.

Synchronize Data on Your Palm

To synchronize a Palm connected to either the desktop or the network through another PC, insert it into the cradle, and press the HotSync button on the cradle's base. If you are using a dial-up connection, do the following:

1. On the Palm, select Applications.

2. Select HotSync.

3. Select Modem. This will dial the modem and synchronize the two computers.

You should find that your contact information, schedules, and tasks are synchronized between the Palm and the desktop.

Synchronize Data on Your Windows CE Device

No matter how you connect a Windows CE device, you can use the same approach to synchronization:

1. Double-click Mobile Devices on the PC desktop.

2. Choose File from the menu.

3. Click Communications.

4. Click the AutoConnect button.

5. Click At All Times (I Plan to Use My COM Port Only for Connecting to My Mobile Device).

Now when you connect the Windows CE device to your network, the Mobile Devices software will automatically synchronize your data.

You can also manually synchronize the two computers, but this requires a direct connection because you can only start the process from the desktop. Select Tools from the menu, and choose Synchronize Now.

Synchronize Organizer Information with Harmony

Hand-helds have special synchronization features for Outlook, Schedule+, or Palm's desktop software. If you use other products, such as Lotus Notes or Organizer, NetManage EccoPro, Act!, and Goldmine, don't think you need to change your software for the convenience of synchronization. Harmony, by Extended Systems, will maintain all your organizer information, keeping the laptop and desktop in sync.

You need Harmony on the desktop because the program downloads the necessary software to your handheld. As with the native handheld synchronization software, you can decide to keep contacts, calendar, tasks, or e-mail updated. Harmony adds a Synchronization Now menu item to your desktop software. You can also use the software with either a cable or a network connection.

To install the evalution version of Harmony, install the program with the user interface on the CD accompanying this book, or install manually by double-clicking the file setup.exe in the directory \Connect to Network on the Run\Harmony\ on the CD.

Synchronize Data between Your Laptop or Notebook and Your Home Network

Notebooks and laptop computers have less built-in support for synchronization, but it is just as important an issue. Because Windows 95, 98, and NT portables do not have the single synchronization programs you find in handhelds, you have to pull together a solution. If you use Windows 98, luckily, some of the software you need comes with the operating system.

Put Your Files into Your Briefcase

Briefcase lets you synchronize files automatically through a special folder. When you put files into the Briefcase folder, the two systems decide which copy is the latest. If you have changed both versions, Briefcase can even detect this. If the application associated with the files supports the feature, Briefcase can call a special *reconciliation handler*. This software, which must come from the application vendor, can actually *merge* two versions of files, getting all your changes in. To accomplish this, you should install Briefcase on both systems:

1. Click Start ➢ Settings ➢ Control Panel. Double-click Add-Remove Programs.

2. Select the Windows Setup tab. Click Accessories in the Components list. Then click details.

3. Click Briefcase in the Accessories dialog box. Click OK.

Briefcase now appears as an icon on your desktop. You are ready to synchronize files between your portable and your network.

For example, you are on the way to work and want to be sure you have the latest versions of your work files. Here are the steps to take:

1. Double-click the Briefcase icon on your portable. Move copies of the work files on that system into that Briefcase.

2. Double-click the Briefcase icon on one of the networked PCs. Move the versions of your work files from the network into the Briefcase.

3. Connect the two computers with a cable.

When you connect the computers, Windows 98 manages the file synchronization.

WARNING As the above steps imply, the files or copies of them have to be in the Briefcase folder to be synchronized. Also, be sure the two computers are set to the same date and time, because this information helps determine synchronization.

Use Your Network to Deliver Entertainment

There are few things as entertaining as, well, as entertainment. If you have thought of networks as the dry stuff of propeller-heads with too much time on their hands, you are in for a surprise. The bits and bytes that make up a network can represent many things, including

- Radio stations, both regular broadcast and Internet radio
- Cable and broadcast television
- Music recorded on CDs
- Videos of popular movies
- TV shows recorded on a VCR to play later
- Digital photographs

Just as you can put word-processing documents and spreadsheets on a server and have access to them from any PC on your network, you can keep video and audio on the network. Although you can play audio and video on stand-alone PCs, you would have to duplicate all the files you want to play, wasting lots of hard-drive space.

Multinational corporations have realized for years that all types of entertainment can be put on a computer. Isn't it time you realized that *you* can put all this on your network *today*? That's what this part of the book is about. Your network can become an entertainment backbone, delivering all sorts of electronic fun wherever you want.

27 Turn Your Networked Computers into Entertainment Stations

Most people think of entertainment equipment as televisions, VCRs, speakers, and stereos. But computers comprise the *real* entertainment centers in your house. Besides using the Internet and a word processor, a PC can let you play television station broadcasts, movies on DVD, audio CDs, and all types of music online. All this comes with high-quality video and even surround-sound.

The biggest advantage you get in turning networked computers into entertainment stations is bringing entertainment to any room in the house. Do you want to watch a movie in the bedroom? Drop a title into the DVD player in your office computer and play it over the network.

Turning your computers into a home entertainment center is a lot easier than you may think. But you do have to start by making sure the computers on your network have the right stuff.

Get a PC Ready for Video

Sure, you can watch video that is delivered over the Internet, and Windows comes with media players, but you can also watch recorded videos and even broadcast or cable television on your PCs. A modern computer provides the graphics for rendering a crisp picture, but it is missing a few things:

- ◆ Computers and televisions work with different types of video signals. They're not built to play television signals.

- ◆ PCs don't come with television tuners, so they have no way of singling out the particular channel you want to watch.

- ◆ Movies that come on DVD disks are compressed so they can fit on a single disk. They use industry standard technologies called MPEG and MPEG-2. PCs typically don't come equipped with the hardware or software needed to play such files.

To play commercial video, the PC needs additional equipment to process television signals, tune channels, and play compressed video.

Install a Tuner Card

Luckily, you can find all the functions you need on a single television tuner card. There are a number of manufacturers of these cards, including ATI and Hauppauge. Besides seeing the video picture, you can do things such as view closed captions and even zoom in on the picture.

NOTE I use an ATI-TV Wonder board. If you want to save even more space, ATI has a combination television-display and video-adapter card, which will also run the regular PC video display. That way, you replace the video board and save the other slots, in case room is tight.

These boards typically support only newer versions of Windows, so you are out of luck if you want to convert an older computer into a television. Because all three platforms support Plug-and-Play hardware, adding a television card to your PC is straightforward. Here are steps that work with an ATI-TV Wonder board:

1. Turn off the PC, and unplug it.
2. Open the PC's case.
3. Find an open slot.

NOTE Some TV tuner cards replace the older video card. If this is the case, remove the older video card during this step.

4. Remove the tab on the case that blocks that slot.
5. Insert the card.
6. A small cable runs from your CD to your PC's soundboard. Remove the connector from the soundboard, and move it to the ATI Wonder board.
7. Use the included jumper cable to run from the CD sound-out socket on the ATI board to the CD sound input on your sound card.
8. Close the case.
9. Plug the PC back in, and turn it on.

WARNING Because you may have multiple sources of audio, such as the output of a sound card or an internal modem, it can be tricky arranging things so you hear everything you want. Check out "Get a PC Ready for Audio" in this section.

When Windows detects the new card, it will display a wizard to install the drivers. Follow the vendor's directions. Now that the card is in place, you have an interesting choice: you can either display television on your computer or display the computer's usual screen on a television.

Display Video on a Computer Monitor

The main reason to display video on a computer monitor is convenience. If you have a PC someplace, you simply don't need a television. Because the computers are on your network, they can take advantage of network resources, such as DVD drives and even video stored on servers.

If you choose to use your computer monitor to display video, there are a few points to remember. Video is especially taxing on your computer display. The more powerful your computer's graphics card, the better the quality of picture you will see. If you have a low-end card, consider replacing it with an *accelerator* card. This is a graphics card with additional circuitry to speed up and enhance the display.

WARNING Be sure that your monitor can support the image offered by the graphics card. Some features of a graphics card, such as screen resolution, need a monitor capable of taking advantage of them. Most new digital monitors support higher resolutions.

Connect Your PC to a Television

With a board like the ATI-TV Wonder, you can also use a television screen like a computer monitor. Why, you might ask, would you use a computer to show a video image on a television? Here are some reasons:

◆ A television can provide a large display that would cost you an arm and a leg if sold as a computer monitor.

◆ A computer provides many capabilities not found in the television, including some tricks you can do with storing video or even taking clips from it and editing it.

◆ By combining the computer with the television, you eliminate the need for the monitor, which means you save both the electrical outlet and the space needed by the monitor.

◆ If you connect your TV to a networked PC, you've suddenly made your TV part of your network.

Certainly, you don't want to buy televisions for every computer you have. Instead, think about putting a PC near the television in an entertainment room. Suddenly you can do things such as watch a movie and, without leaving the room, go to the Internet to settle an argument about one of the actors in the film.

With a television tuner card, making a PC work with a television is easy. All you do is take a standard cable for television, connect one end to the television tuner card, and connect the other end to the television.

Hook Up the Video in the Right Sequence

The only tricky part of making video work on your PC is hooking everything in the right sequence. You need a video source for the tuner card. This might be a cable television signal, an antenna, or the output of a VCR.

Whether you use the computer monitor to see the video or to send it to a television, follow these steps:

1. If you want to use a VCR with a particular PC, run a cable from the VCR's output to the tuner card's input.

2. The video source plugs into the VCR's input. This source is either an antenna or the cable system. If the VCR does not directly accept cable television, connect the output of the cable box to the VCR's input.

3. If you aren't using a VCR, run the television source directly to the tuner card's input.

4. If you are using the computer monitor to display the video, you are set.

5. To use a television as the computer's monitor, run a cable from the tuner card's output to the television's input.

By following these steps, you should avoid accidentally cutting a piece of equipment out of the video path. Next, you need to put the sound in place, and you should be set.

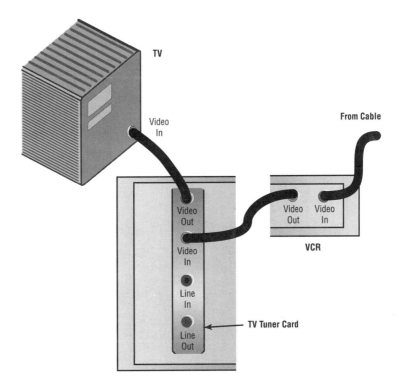

Get a PC Ready for Audio

What's the sense of having wonderful video if the audio sounds like a cat in heat sitting in an old steel garbage can? There are plenty of reasons to have good audio for your computers, especially because you can store music and more on your network:

◆ Have great sound with videos.

◆ Listen to your favorite CDs.

◆ Download music from the Internet.

◆ Add decibels of destruction to your computer gaming.

Instead of a single speaker, or even a pair, your computer might drive a powerful set of speakers from tweeters to subwoofers. To ensure good listening, you have to consider the PC's sound card, the speakers you use, and the way you hook everything together.

Install a Sound Card

Virtually all computers today come with sound—either a sound card or sound support built into the motherboard. And although that may be plenty for your tastes, some new advances might make an audiophile consider purchasing a new sound card.

One development has been 3-D sound, in which a program can make sound seem like it's coming from anywhere around you, including behind, above, or below. Another advancement has been DVD video that comes with multiple-channel, Dolby sound. The only way to get the full effect is to purchase a sound card that supports it.

There are a number of vendors—including Diamond Multimedia, Turtle Beach, Yamaha, and Creative Labs, which developed the original Sound Blaster card—that make higher-end sound cards. There are four things to consider, though:

- ◆ The cards run $100 or more, so if audio doesn't grab you, invest the money elsewhere.

- ◆ High-end sound cards require PCI slots, rather than the ISA slots used by earlier cards.

- ◆ Many of the cards are twice as thick as other cards, meaning that while they only use one PCI slot, they will take up two spaces.

- ◆ If you want surround-sound for a DVD movie, you need additional speakers.

If you install a sound card, move it as far from the PC's video card as possible, because you can get electrical noise and interference that lowers the quality of the sound.

Pick the Speakers

You need speakers to pick up the signal from the sound card, whether a brand new one or an older model. There's an incredible variety available:

- ◆ Most computers come with speakers. Don't count them out, as some provide thoroughly decent sound, such as the JBL Pro speakers that can come with a Compaq Presario.

◆ A number of vendors, such as Cambridge SoundWorks and LabTec, have three-part units that place a speaker to either side and a sub-woofer in the middle to increase the richness of the sound.

◆ Some companies are bringing leading-edge speaker design to the PC. Benwin, for example, offers the BW2000, a flat-panel speaker system with a subwoofer.

Whatever type of speaker you use, don't rely on the amplifier built into the sound card; use speakers with their own amplifiers. The reason is that the sound-card amplifiers are often inadequate.

If you already have a stereo amplifier, you could give yourself a boost by running a cable from the line-out jack on the sound card to the line-in on the amplifier. You now have the power to drive larger speakers and fill a room with sound—important for a TV room or home theater.

Hook the Audio Together

The bus in your PC can pass many types of signals back and forth, but sound isn't one of them. For that reason, you usually have to connect the audio card with other devices in a PC to get all of the sound that might arise to the speakers. Otherwise, you could totally cut out a device that you want to hear.

Here are some steps that will help:

1. The sound card line-out always goes to either the powered speakers or an amplifier.

2. Realize what other devices might need access to a speaker. A modem, for example, has a line-out jack so you can hear the device dial out. TV tuner cards also have audio that you might want to route through the sound card.

3. Make a list of the different sound sources you need to integrate, and then decide how to chain them together. You might need one cable to run from the modem sound-out to a television tuner sound-in. Then the sound-out from the TV tuner would run into the line-in of the sound card.

4. If you listen to music while going online and the amplified sound of an internal modem grates your nerves, leave it out of the chain. The modem has its own speaker, so you will still hear a muffled acknowl-edgment that your computer is happily shaking hands with another computer.

5. Cable the cards together, and then run a cable from the output of the sound card to either the powered speakers or external amplifier.

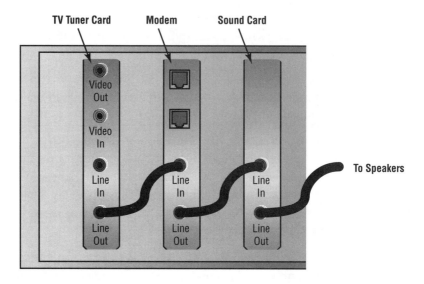

Once you have cabled the PC sound sources in a workable chain, you are ready to hear anything your computer can throw at you.

Get a PC Ready for Games

Much of the set-up to let a PC play audio and video also supports computer gaming, which is good, because a network can support multiple people playing each other on the same game. Given the advanced state of game graphics, you should put more emphasis on the computer's video card. Consider one that will provide both 2-D and 3-D acceleration. A sound card that supports 3-D sound will also add to your gaming experience.

An additional piece of hardware you might want is a joystick. There's a reason that joysticks sell—they make it easier to play the games. Between the video and audio cards, you probably have a "gaming port," which is otherwise known as the place to connect the joystick.

NOTE   If anyone in your house uses a Sony PlayStation, a product called bleem!, from bleem, LLC, can let you run PlayStation games on your PC.

28 Put Your Audio on an MP3 Server

MP3 has become the hottest thing to hit audio in a long time. The reason is that MP3 is a technology that lets people record audio—whether music, speech, or even pure sound—in relatively small files with nearly perfect fidelity. Because it is a computer file format, you can download music, transfer it from one computer to the next, and even load it onto portable MP3 players.

The qualities of MP3 make it perfect for use in your home network. You can create, relatively easily, an MP3 audio server in your home that provides great benefits:

- ◆ You can centrally store all sorts of audio and play it on any computer in the house.

- ◆ Copy a music CD in an MP3 format to a networked hard drive so you have easy access.

- ◆ Record an audio book in MP3, and then continue listening as you move from one room to the other.

- ◆ There are free MP3 players for both PCs and Macs, so no one need feel left out.

- ◆ Download MP3 music from the Internet, and listen to new groups and types of music without paying for full CDs, sound unheard.

- ◆ Copy music from your server to a portable player.

Because MP3 audio consists of computer files, it's no harder to store than spreadsheets. You need to set up disk space in a server and then use software to record and organize your collection of sound.

Create Your MP3 Server

Creating an MP3 server really is the same as setting up a shared directory. Choose a drive on your network and create a directory, perhaps called Music. Decide whether everyone will be able to record songs and add information about recordings or whether that should be done only at one PC. (See "9. Set Up the Network Software.") It's a trade-off between letting everyone participate and being sure that people won't start erasing tracks, either accidentally or in disgust with someone else's taste.

Plan on plenty of disk space in the server. You have a choice in the quality of MP3 recording, with higher quality using more disk space. Even if you restrict yourself to a level better than what you would hear on FM radio but not quite up to CD sound, a music recording will take about 1 megabyte of space per minute of sound. That means a typical music CD could take 40 to 50 megabytes of space. Have 100 CDs? That's 4 to 5 gigabytes. Speech is a better byte bargain, at several megabytes per minute, but it is still expansive.

Pick Your Recording and Cataloging Software

Once the hard-drive space is set aside, you need some software, both to record music and organize it. A good program is MusicMatch Jukebox from MusicMatch (www.musicmatch.com). This sophisticated software can record in a variety of formats, including MP3 and WAV. It has some spectacular capabilities:

- ◆ It keeps all your recordings automatically organized by artist, album, and cut.

- ◆ It ties in to CDDB (CD database), an Internet information service, to automatically enter information about many CDs.

- ◆ It adds information about tempos, moods, genres, and preferences to selections.

- ◆ It plays entire CDs or lets you pick groups of selections based on various criteria.

- ◆ It records CDs or connects other audio sources, such as tapes and phonographs, to the line-in jack of the sound card and record them.

- ◆ An included equalizer lets you adjust audio levels to your liking.

The product is shareware, so you can try a restricted version and then purchase if you like it. A registered version allows you to record at CD quality, whereas the shareware version restricts you to near-CD quality.

Installation is easy:

1. Install the program with the user interface on the CD accompanying this book, or install manually by double-clicking the file mmjb41056.exe in the directory \Network Delivers Entertainment\MusicMatch\ on the CD.

2. MusicMatch Jukebox stores music in its own directory, which defaults to C:\Program Files\MusicMatch. Be sure when prompted to specify the network directory you are using as your MP3 server.

3. If you want to maintain the recording collection from more than one PC, you must install the software at each machine. Each time, provide the proper network location.

4. From one of the computers, start MusicMatch. Choose Music Library from the Options menu. Click New to create a new music library, which is a database of music selections and information about them.

NOTE You can create multiple music libraries for different people in your home.

The program is now installed and you are ready to begin recording. Converting a music source to MP3 is the same as using a tape-recorder interface:

1. Select Start ➤ MusicMatch ➤ MusicMatch Jukebox.

2. Select the Options menu, then choose Recorder, and then Source. Pick the appropriate music source.

3. Click the round, red button on the jukebox to be sure the Recorder is visible.

4. Check which titles you wish to record.

5. Click the triangular button on the Recorder to start the recording process.

As you record more, you can start putting tracks into *playlists,* to help speed your choices of music to the speakers. Be sure to read the help file and experiment with the software to see what it can do.

There are two other types of software you should consider, both of which are free. One is MP3 DataBase. This product creates databases of collections of music. Some of its functions include

♦ Searching through music entries

♦ Making changes to groups of cuts, such as updating the artist's name

♦ Finding and eliminating duplicate entries

It's like feeding your CDs into an elaborate spreadsheet—one that can comfortably reside on your MP3 server so everyone can use it.

 To install MP3 DataBase, do the following:

1. Install the program with the user interface on the CD accompanying this book, or install manually by double-clicking the file Setup.exe in the directory \Network Delivers Entertainment\MP3 Database\ on the CD.

2. When the install wizard starts, click Next, then click Browse, and find a directory on the MP3 server.

3. Follow the software's directions to finish the installation.

MP3 DataBase is now ready to use. Because MP3 is so popular, there are many other programs available. One that will be useful is an MP3 player for the computers on your network, so they can play the audio tracks. A good one is the RealPlayer G2, and again it's free. There are versions for both Windows and the Macintosh.

To install RealPlayer G2 for Windows, do the following:

1. Copy the file `r32_g20_4med.exe` from the CD accompanying this book to the PC's hard drive.

2. Highlight the file in Windows Explorer or My Computer on the desktop.

3. Follow the instructions for installing the software.

The computer will now play MP3 files as well as sites that provide RealAudio content over the Internet. Continue to install the RealPlayer G2 on all the other PCs, and you will be able to play music anywhere on the network. For a Macintosh player, go to `www.realplayer.com`.

29 Find Music on the Internet

Not only can you record music from CDs but there are many sites on the Internet that have MP3 files you can download directly to your server. Some of the sites that have music are the following:

◆ MP3.com (`www.mp3.com`) is a site that has information on MP3 as well as many titles you can download.

◆ 2Look4.com (`www.2look4.com`) and MP3Bot (`www.informatch.com/mediabot`) are MP3 search engines where you can look for music.

◆ Dimension Music (`www.dimensionmusic.com`) is a site where many musicians sell their work in an MP3 format.

When you find an MP3 selection you like, you might want to put it into your music catalog. Add an MP3 file with MusicMatch this way:

1. Download the file from an Internet site. Save it to your MP3 server.

2. Start MusicMatch.

3. Choose File from the Options menu. Click on Add New Track to Music Library.

4. Highlight the correct directory in the left window pane, and then choose the files you are adding in the right pane. Click OK.

The files are now in your music catalog, and you can search for them and build playlists of music.

WARNING   MP3 music on the Internet is not necessarily free to use however you want. You may have to buy titles, or there may be restrictions on their use.

30 Get Information on CDs from the Web to Your Network's MP3 Server

As you record CDs onto your network's MP3 server, you will want to enter the names of the artists, the album, and the track. You can enter the information in MusicMatch Jukebox by hand, but there is a better way.

CDDB is a database of information on thousands of CDs. It doesn't cost anything and will work with MusicMatch Jukebox, or with RealJukebox from RealNetworks for that matter, to automatically fill in the information.

To use CDDB with MusicMatch Jukebox, do the following:

1. Start MusicMatch Jukebox.

2. Under the Options menu, click on Settings.

3. Select the CDDB Preferences tab.

4. Be sure there is a check next to Enable CDDB CD Lookup Service.

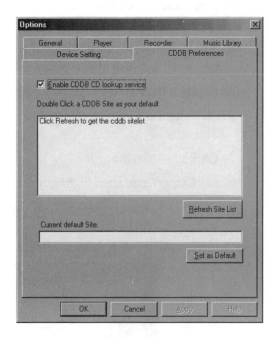

When you add MP3 titles to a music catalog, be sure your Internet connection is on. When you add a CD, CDDB will provide the information if available. Otherwise, you will have to add the names by hand.

31 Bring Music from Your Network with You Wherever You Go

When your music collection is online, you can pull together collections of tracks from your server and bring them with you. All you need is a portable MP3 player, such as the Diamond Multimedia Rio.

The Rio is about the size of a small transistor radio and comes with headphones. A special connector, also included, attaches to the parallel port of a PC. The cable will still connect to the computer so the PC can still use a printer or some other device that attaches to the parallel port. You connect a cable from the parallel connector to the Rio.

You can get support for either Windows or the Mac. The Rio comes with software that will download MP3 files from your server. Here's how to do it:

1. Connect the Rio to the parallel port connector.

2. Start the Rio software. Click Start ➤ Programs ➤ RipPMP300 ➤ Rio Manager.

3. Click the Mem button.

4. Click Open, and then highlight the tracks you want to download.

5. Click Open again, and then click the Download button, and the music will download to the Rio.

Now you can take any combination of music tracks you want. There are only 34 MB of memory in the Rio, so you will only get about half an hour of near–CD quality audio, more if you drop the quality. To fit more music, you can get a flash memory card that will fit into the Rio.

32 Play Radio from the Internet

If you want to listen to music and people talking, you don't have to turn on a desk radio. The Internet has tremendous numbers of radio stations available from all over the world, and with a home network—especially with high-speed Internet access—everyone can have their own choice. There are both stations that only work on the Internet, and normal stations that provide Internet content in addition to their broadcasts. They *stream* audio, which is a way of sending compressed sound in chunks over the Internet. You use special software that recognizes the formats and converts them to sound that plays over a sound card. Two of the popular formats are

- RealAudio from RealNetwork (`www.realnetwork.com`), with the free RealPlayer G2

- LiquidAudio (`www.liquidaudio.com`), with the free Liquid Player

With a connection between your network and the Internet—especially with a high bandwidth connection—you can bring world radio to any computer in your home. Even with a 56K modem, the quality equals that of most FM stations.

Tuning in the Internet

From New Orleans rhythm and blues to techno and even Gaelic music, you can find almost anything among the growing number of stations on the Internet. Here are some sources for both Internet-only stations and traditional stations that also broadcast on the Internet:

- NetRadio (`www.netradio.com`) offers a range of specialty music channels. Many of its channels appear as Presets on the RealAudio G2 player, but don't be alarmed if some are not to be found. Net-Radio apparently has reorganized its offerings, but RealAudio G2 hasn't necessarily kept up.

- About.com (`internetradio.about.com`) is an information service that, among other things, covers Internet radio. It also has a newsletter with information on stations and has an extensive set of links to stations around the world.

- Broadcast.com (`www.broadcast.com`) offers a central point to catch many commercial stations around the country.

Actually tuning in any of the stations is easy. You need to have a player for whatever format they use, but each site typically offers a link to get a free player. Here's how to listen:

1. If you haven't done so before, download the software to work with your browser.

2. Highlight the file in the Windows Explorer, and double-click it, and then follow the vendor's installation instructions.

3. Use your browser to surf to a radio station that catches your eye— or ear.

4. Click on the audio link.

You can now enjoy music, news, and discussions from almost anywhere in the world to any networked computer in your home.

33 Add TV to a Home Network

If you want to take a break from the computer and watch some TV, you can do that without shifting position. There are four basic sources of television that might interest you:

- ◆ Broadcast
- ◆ VCR videos
- ◆ DVD videos
- ◆ Internet-streamed video

Depending on your interests and the set-up of your network, any of the four may interest you. However, to use any of the first three, you need to outfit the computers on your network with a television tuner card. (See "27. Turn Your Networked Computers into Entertainment Stations.")

Streamed video only requires a software player; however, unless you have a high-capacity connection to the Internet, the video will seem jerky and highly unsatisfying. If you still want to give it a shot, the RealPlayer G2 will show video, and you can find sites at www.broadcast.com, among other locations.

Combine Broadcast TV and VCR Video with Your Network

Broadcast television means either traditionally transmitted signals or cable. Although you can play these on your computer, there is a catch: you won't be able to send it across your network. Unfortunately, the vast majority of broadcast television uses *analog* signals that simply won't mix with your network, which is why you need to use special hardware to receive it in the first place. Even most cable television uses analog signals.

What you can do, though, is pull television cable through the house as you might pull network cable. The goal would be to have a cable outlet near every computer location you have. Feeding into the cable would be either an antenna or a cable-television signal. Then all you do is run a short cable from the wall to the TV tuner card in the PC.

Another choice would be to connect the cable running through the house to the video-out connector on a VCR—the one that would typically connect to the television set. Now you can feed a signal from the VCR throughout the house.

Play DVD Video over Your Network

Fortunately, you will have a much easier time playing DVD video over your network. Here's how to do it:

1. If you don't have one already, install a DVD drive on your network server.

2. Ensure that all other computers will have access to that drive.

3. Put a movie in the DVD drive.

4. Go to the computer on which you want to watch the video.

5. Start the TV tuner software, and open the networked DVD drive as the video source.

You can watch the video full screen, if you want, or reduce the window, and do other things at the same time. One hint about performance: if the video seems jerky at all, try shrinking its window a bit, and the picture should smooth out.

34 Store Video on Your Network

Wouldn't it be great to have video on your own server, to play anywhere on your network? If that's what you think, then you should be happy to know that you can start doing this today. Here are some of the things a video server lets you do:

◆ Capture television programs centrally, and then replay them anywhere at home.

◆ Move home video onto a server where you can digitally edit it.

◆ Save wear and tear on videotapes.

The trick is storing digital formats of video on a network file server. It's as though you copied video from DVD disks to a hard drive. But you can digitize VCR movies and home videos with the right equipment. That means a *frame grabber,* which is a board that can translate analog video—the type you get from a VCR or television station—into a digital format for storage. A frame grabber can capture single frames, continuous video, and sound, to boot. TV tuners such as the ATI-TV Wonder card have frame grabbers built-in, so if you are set up to see video on a computer, you don't need additional equipment.

More of a problem is the amount of space that digital video needs: about several gigabytes for a two-and-one-quarter-hour movie. Unlike MP3 files, which you might reasonably have in overabundant supply, your network server probably has limited room for videos. As hard-drive capacity increases, and the cost of those same drives decreases, it will become more practical to store digital video on your home network server. Until then, you might just have to settle for storing only your favorite movie.

Store Your Video

Even if you are cramped for space, you can still store video. What you need is

◆ A video source, whether a TV, VCR, or DVD player

◆ A video capture card, probably in the form of a TV tuner card

◆ Recording software that accompanies the TV tuner card

◆ A high-bandwidth network, such as 10/100 BaseT

With these items, you will be able to transfer data from the video source, through the capture card, to the networked hard drive. Although the steps will vary, depending on the actual hardware and software you use, here are some general steps:

1. Pick a location on your network server to store the video. You will want a couple of gigabytes for an hour of video.

2. Connect the video source to the line-in connector of the TV tuner card.

3. Follow the software's directions to begin recording. For the ATI-TV Wonder card mentioned before, use the VCR application included with the hardware.

4. Start the video source, and record it.

After the video has run its course, stop the recording software. You can now play the video through the TV tuner cards in the PCs on your network.

35 Create Your Own CDs

It's never been easier to make your own CDs. You can create music disks or even move files to store off your system. To record CDs, you need a CD recorder as well as software to do the recording. With a network, the CD recorder lets you extend the reach of your file servers anywhere you can carry a CD.

While once there was great complexity and preparation needed for CD recording, the process has become one of drag-and-drop for many products.

NOTE There are two types of CD recording formats: record once only and rerecordable. Get the latter, as it supports both types and lets you reuse the special rerecordable media—which is as handy as an eraser on the end of a pencil.

Here's how to start making your own CD:

1. Install the CD writer. Although you can get external models, only do so if you want to run a SCSI adapter card. Otherwise, get an internal IDE model and replace the CD drive in one of your PCs. Because the writer will also read CDs, you lose no capabilities.

2. Install the software according to the vendor's instructions.

3. Choose the material you want to record. Realize that if you want to put music on a CD, you shouldn't plan on it being MP3 tracks, as most CD drives cannot handle that format.

4. Put the material together in a directory on your network. Modern CD recorders may not require you to copy all the material at the same time, but you will lose track if you have one file here and another there.

5. Format a blank CD disk according to the vendor's instructions.

6. Follow the vendor's instructions for how to record to the CD.

NOTE Some software, such as what came with my Hewlett-Packard CD Writer Plus 8210i, will allow you to add things to a CD by dragging and dropping the files onto the CD drive.

Not all CD drives can read the rewritable format, so don't use it if you may need to play a CD on an older drive. If you have problems with the CD recorder and want access to something on one of the CDs you have recorded, you will require a newer drive compatible with the rewritable format.

WARNING Although you can, for your personal use, record music from one CD onto another, don't give a CD with music to someone else; otherwise you might one day receive a visit from a disgruntled music company's lawyer.

Connect Your Network to the Outside World

People may be amazed at what the Internet offers, but dialing in from a PC pales in comparison to connecting your home network to the outside world. Here are just some of the options:

◆ Save money by sharing one Internet connection with everyone at home.

◆ Make money by running your own e-commerce site.

◆ Have your own Web server without monthly ISP maintenance charges.

◆ Have as many e-mail accounts as you need with your own e-mail server.

◆ Protect kids at home from the Internet's dangers.

◆ Let children collaborate on schoolwork with neighbors over your network.

Some of your choices—such as running a Web or e-mail server—may be a little challenging, but they are achievable with a little patience. The others are surprisingly easy to learn.

36 Connect Your Network to the Internet at High Speed

You could take back roads from your network to the Internet, but a highway is much faster. The first step from your network to a wider world is a high-speed connection to the Internet.

Although you can share an Internet connection and an e-mail account on a regular dial-up line, higher bandwidth means browsers work faster, even with several people surfing the Web at the same time. In some cases, it also means a link that is always running, so you can literally host your own Internet site, including full Web services. Better yet, in many cases, the costs are fairly modest.

Your Service Options

There are different types of higher-speed Internet connections:

◆ ISDN

◆ Cable

◆ DSL

◆ Satellite

◆ The use of two phone lines at the same time

Each type has its strengths and weaknesses, including cost, capacity, availability, and what it can do. The combination of your local service providers, ISP, and even the location of your home may rule out some of these choices.

There two types of equipment: that which connects directly to your LAN and that which attaches directly to a PC. You can then make the modem available to any other PC on the network. (See "37. Share Your Internet Connection over the Network.")

Use ISDN for Your Internet Connection

ISDN—or *integrated services digital network*—is a special service that may be available from your phone company. Though it uses regular phone lines, it provides a digital connection that gives you

◆ Two independent communication channels

◆ Two independent telephone numbers

◆ The ability to make regular phone or fax calls on either channel

◆ The ability to have two calls going on at the same time

◆ The ability to combine the two channels into a single, high-speed data connection

This means you can make a phone call while someone on your network is using the same line to dial-up an Internet connection. If you run an office at home, you can receive a fax while online. You can also sometimes *bond* the two communications channels into one. Because each alone offers a 64Kbps connection, which is faster than any dial-up, you can get up to

128Kbps bandwidth, which translates into sending or receiving a 1MB file in about a minute.

All of this may sound great, but there are some drawbacks:

◆ Your ISP has to support ISDN connections, which means a phone call to the ISP before you place an order with the phone company.

◆ Some phone companies charge a monthly fee above ordinary telephone line costs: not only a monthly rate but a *per minute per channel* rate for usage. Even at one cent a minute, the costs can add up. If your Internet usage—let alone any other types of calls—was 20 hours a month using both channels for a high-speed connection, the cost would be an extra $24 a month.

◆ There are technical restrictions that may make ISDN unavailable to you, even if available in your general area.

◆ If your electrical power goes out for any reason, you won't be able to use the ISDN line.

To get ISDN, you have to place an order for the service with your local telephone company. ISDN is very different from a regular phone service. You can't directly plug in a regular telephone or fax machine. You can, however, plug phones and fax machines into an ISDN modem, which you will need anyway to dial-up your ISP. You can choose a modem that connects directly to a PC or one that connects to a LAN.

Installing ISDN service is reputedly difficult, but some preparation will see you through the process. The example in this case is the DIVA LAN modem, which comes with a four-port hub and two regular phone connections and so requires an Ethernet network.

Before you start installing any ISDN modem, though, you should have the following information from your telephone company:

◆ The two telephone numbers of your ISDN line

◆ The service provider identifier (SPID) for each phone number

◆ The switch type

Even if your ISDN modem is supposed to automatically configure itself, ask for the information anyway, because the feature does not always work. You also need the following information from your ISP:

◆ Two phone numbers for the ISP's ISDN service

◆ Your username and password

◆ The primary and secondary DNS server's addresses, which are special IP addresses

With this information, you should be able to install the ISDN modem. The following steps are for the DIVA LAN modem. Other ISDN modems will vary in the details, but the basic procedures will be similar.

1. Turn off a PC that you will use to install the modem.

2. Plug the included ISDN cable into both the modem and your ISDN wall jack.

3. Connect the PC to any of the modem's Ethernet ports with a UTP cable supplied with the modem.

4. Connect the power supply to the power jack.

5. Turn on the computer, and install the configuration software. Follow the vendor's directions on how to use the information from the phone company and ISP.

If you plan to use the ISDN line for telephone calls or a fax machine, plug the equipment into the modem's phone jacks. You are now set to use ISDN service.

Use Cable for Your Internet Connection

Many cable television companies are offering connections to the Internet. If available in your area, strongly consider it, because cable connections to the Internet have great advantages:

◆ They may offer the fastest connections to the Internet you can find. Downloading a 1MB file could take as little as 10 seconds!

◆ Such connections are always on, so there's no more dialing, and you can connect to the Internet on a moment's notice.

◆ They are usually reasonably priced, with monthly charges often in the $35 to $45 a month range.

It's clear there are some strong reasons to consider cable modems. However, there are downsides to consider:

◆ You probably have to make your cable company your new ISP, which would mean new e-mail addresses, passwords, and so on.

◆ Cable modem access is not always available as real two-way communications. In this case, you would need a dial-up connection in addition to the cable line.

◆ If too many people are on the same cable trunk line in a given area, such as a large apartment building, the bandwidth can drop.

◆ Cable modem Internet service is currently offered in relatively few places because most cable companies have to upgrade their lines and equipment to support it.

◆ Not all cable modems are created equal. Some cable companies require that you use products from particular vendors.

◆ You may need a 10baseT or 10/100baseT Ethernet network or at least a compatible NIC in a PC to connect an external modem.

The cons, however, are far less compelling than the pros. If you decide to get cable Internet access, you can use the following steps to install a cable modem. The procedure is for a U.S. Robotics CMX external cable modem and a two-way cable connection, but the process should be similar to that for other products:

1. Ask your cable company whether there are any restrictions on the type of cable modem you can use with their service.

2. Buy or lease the cable modem and obtain the MAC (media access control) address. You will need it as you place an order with your cable television company.

3. If this is only a one-way cable connection, you will also need a regular dial-up analog modem.

4. Check that your PC has TCP/IP support installed. Click Start ➢ Settings ➢ Control Panel. Double-click Network.

5. If there is a TCP/IP entry, click OK, and go to step 7.

6. If there is no TCP/IP listing in the window, follow the directions in "19. Let Computers Talk with a Network Protocol" to add a protocol. Use Microsoft as the vendor.

7. Shut down your PC. If it doesn't have a 10baseT or 10/100baseT Ethernet card, install one now.

8. Connect the line from the cable company to the cable modem.

9. Plug one end of the supplied UTP cable into the cable modem and the other end into either your Ethernet hub or a NIC in one of your computers.

10. Connect the modem's power supply. Turn on the modem, and then turn on the PC.

You have now installed the cable modem and are ready to use it. Had the cable connection been only one-way, you would have connected an external analog modem to the cable modem's serial port.

Use DSL for Your Internet Connection

DSL, or *digital subscriber line,* is actually a series of related technologies, including ADSL (asymmetrical DSL) and SDSL (symmetrical DSL). With all of these, the phone company uses special digital technology over existing copper wires, much like ISDN. But there are differences:

◆ DSL provides much higher bandwidth than ISDN, with the ability to download a 1MB file in 10 to 15 seconds. You can get faster rates, as DSL's potential capacity is higher, but it will cost more.

◆ DSL doesn't interfere with your phone line, so you can handle voice or fax traffic at the same time as an Internet connection.

◆ You will typically pay a flat monthly rate for unlimited use, so DSL can be far cheaper than ISDN, with prices, depending on where you are, starting about $50 a month. The local telephone company may charge a premium for the highest connections.

◆ You get a permanent connection to the Internet, so there is no dialing and no waiting.

◆ Even if the power goes out, you can still make a phone call on a DSL line.

Like cable Internet service, DSL makes a compelling argument. And like cable Internet service, there are less positive considerations:

◆ You probably have to switch to your telephone company as the new ISP, which would mean new e-mail addresses, passwords, and so on.

- Like ISDN, DSL requires you to be within a certain distance of the telephone central office, so those in a rural setting may be bucolic but out of luck.

- There are many variations on DSL, and each version needs different equipment, so ordering a modem is trickier than usual.

- DSL service is currently offered in relatively few places, so there's a good chance you won't be able to find it.

- You may need a 10baseT or 10/100baseT Ethernet network or at least a compatible NIC in a PC to connect an external DSL modem.

To install a DSL modem, use the following general steps. They are for an internal DSL modem, but they differ from the steps in using an external modem only in connecting the external modem via an Ethernet cable to either a PC's NIC or an Ethernet network.

1. Get the MAC address from the modem vendor, and provide it to the phone company when setting up your service.

2. Turn off the PC, disconnect the power, and open the case.

3. Insert the DSL modem card into an open PCI slot.

4. Close the case, and connect the modem to the DSL line. Connect a phone or fax, if you plan to use one, to the modem.

5. Turn on the PC.

6. Windows will note the new hardware. Follow the vendor's directions on installing the drivers.

If you had used an external modem, you would have connected the modem, via an Ethernet cable with RJ-45 connectors, to either a NIC on a PC or to your Ethernet hub. You are now set to use your DSL connection.

Use Satellite Technology for Your Internet Connection

Another technology—satellite Internet connections—is making broadband potentially available to many people. Using a service such as DirectPC from Hughes Networks, information from the Internet, such as a Web page or e-mail, is beamed up to the satellite and then relayed to a point on the ground. The advantages are clear:

- You don't need to wait for the telephone or cable company to start offering broadband service in your area.

♦ There are no restrictions on how far you can be from the service provider.

♦ Even though not at the speed of DSL or a cable modem, the download speed of about 350Kbps is almost three times faster than ISDN or fast enough to download a 1MB file in 20 to 30 seconds.

It is an attractive option for those who live away from large population concentrations that might have some of the other broadband offerings. However, there are some drawbacks:

♦ You need a dish antenna, which is a pricey piece of equipment that can run hundreds of dollars.

♦ There has to be a clear southern exposure, so the antenna can be directed to the location of the satellite.

♦ The satellite transmission is one way, so you need an analog modem to send data or browser commands.

♦ The service provider has to become your ISP, which will involve changing e-mail addresses, passwords, and the like.

♦ This is probably the most expensive broadband solution available. Monthly costs are for limited blocks of usage, such as 20 hours.

♦ Unlike services such as DSL and cable, which can be placed on a network without great difficulty, using satellite service from a network requires the participation of the vendor and costs more money.

Installation is totally dependent on the service vendor and will probably require service people to do some of the work, such as mount the antenna.

Using Two Phones

If you can't get some of the broadband connections, such as DSL or cable, it is actually possible to use two analog modems and two phone lines together to get up to a 112Kbps connection to an ISP! It's called *multilink* under Windows 98. The advantages are clear:

♦ You get faster transmission than with a single modem.

♦ All you need are two phone lines and a modem. There's no need to wait for special service offerings.

♦ You get a choice of ISPs.

At the same time, there are some real limitations on using multilink connections:

◆ The 112Kbps rate is the best possible, but that depends on a perfect phone connection, which you will almost never find. A more realistic level to expect might be about 90 to 100Kbps.

◆ Although you can use analog modems with a multilink connection, it was really designed for ISDN modems. Analog modems can cause errors that slow the connection.

◆ Multilink is part of Windows 98 Dial-Up Networking (DUN) and won't work with other communications programs. Luckily, browsers or e-mail readers, such as Outlook and Eudora, use DUN.

◆ As with other technologies, you have to be sure that your ISP supports multilink as well as PPP, or Point-to-Point Protocol.

◆ At least one of the modems must be a model that specifically supports multilink.

If you want to set up a multilink connection, first install both modems, and then follow these steps:

1. Click Start ➤ Programs ➤ Accessories ➤ Communications ➤ Dial-Up.

2. Double-click Make New Connection.

3. Type in a name for the connection.

4. Under Select a Device, choose the modem that has multilink support. Click Next.

5. Type a telephone number for your ISP, and click Finish.

6. Go to the Dial-Up Networking folder, and highlight the connection you just created.

7. Right-click and select Properties.

8. Select the Multilink tab.

9. Click Use additional devices, and then click Add.

10. In Edit Extra Device, choose the second modem, and click OK.

You have now set up the two modems to work with the connection you created. Configure your e-mail and browser programs to use this connection, and you will obtain the benefits of multilink.

37 Share Your Internet Connection over the Network

One of the great advantages of a high-bandwidth connection to the Internet when you have a home network is sharing that connection with all the PCs in your home.

Once you have a connection set up, sharing it generally involves getting a *proxy server*. Think of how you can check your e-mail and use a browser at the same time on one computer. A proxy server is software or special hardware that connects to your ISP and manages multiple users across your network.

If you are using phone line, power line, or wireless networking, chances are strong that the kit you bought comes with proxy server software. In this case, go ahead and follow the vendor's directions for installing and using it.

 You can also use a third-party product. Lovdahl Consulting makes a software proxy server called Webetc, with versions for home and small office users. These versions limit the number of people who can use the connection at one time to three and five, respectively, but that should be plenty for most home uses. Here's how to install it:

1. Install the program with the user interface on the CD accompanying this book, or install manually by double-clicking the file SetupStd.exe in the directory \Connect Network to Outside\Webetc\ on the CD.

2. When asked to reboot the system, click Yes.

3. After rebooting, click Start ➤ Programs ➤ Webetc ➤ Launch Webetc Gateway.

4. Select My Internet Connection is through Dial-Up if you use a dial-up connection. Under Internet Dial-Up Connection to Use, choose the connection you normally use.

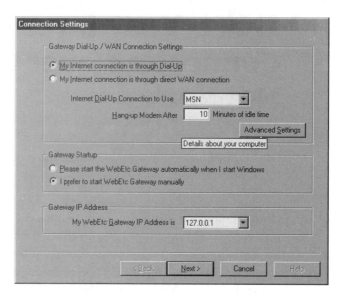

5. Select My Internet Connection Is through Direct WAN Connection if you use either a direct cable or DSL modem.

6. Don't modify the IP address shown. Click Next.

7. You need to supply the SMTP Mail Server Address, POP3 Mail Server Address, and NNTP News Server Address, all available from your ISP.

8. Click Finish.

You can now share the Internet link on the PC with any other PC on your home network. For more information, right-click the Webetc logo in the system tray, choose Configure, and click the More Info tab. There is a tutorial and a manual, and there are helpful troubleshooting tips, as well.

There are also hardware proxy servers, such as the Multi-Tech MTPSR1 ProxyServer. They connect an external modem directly to an Ethernet network without tying up the resources of a PC and requiring the PC to be on at all times. This solution can make sense if you have older computers and don't want to tax them by channeling all the Internet traffic through them.

Once your proxy server is set, you need to direct the browsers and e-mail software on each PC so you can use your LAN to connect to your ISP. As an example, here's how you would set Outlook Express:

1. Select Accounts from the Tools menu.

2. Click the Mail tab, and highlight your e-mail service.

3. Click the Properties key.

4. Select the Connection tab.

5. Select Connect Using My Local Area Network (LAN), and click OK.

6. Click Close. You may have to stop and then restart Outlook Express for the change to take place.

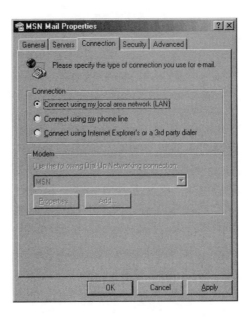

By making these changes, Outlook Express will now look to the proxy server for your Internet connection. You can configure other e-mail readers similarly.

To have Internet Explorer use the proxy server, use this procedure:

1. Choose Internet Options from the View menu.

2. Select the Connection tab.

3. Click "Connect to the Internet Using a Local Area Network", and click OK.

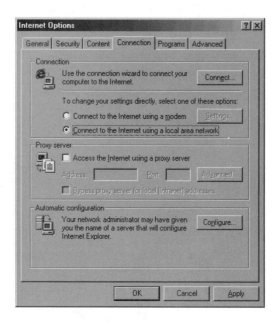

Now when you want to use the Web, Internet Explorer will use the proxy server instead of starting a dial-up connection.

38 Connect Your Network to the Internet

If you thought the Internet was amazing the first time you used a Web browser, try turning one of your PCs into an Internet host! Some of the things you can do are

- ◆ Have your own domain name for your business or enjoyment.

- ◆ Create as many e-mail addresses as you want.

- ◆ Create a Web site for your neighborhood.

- ◆ Run an e-commerce store out of your house.

Having your own Internet node gives you complete control over how your domain runs and what happens on it. It will take some work, but you can do it with a little patience. Here are three steps to having your own Internet site:

1. Get the right ISP and connection.

2. Apply for your domain name.

3. Prepare a server.

With these steps, you will have your own presence on the Internet.

Get the Right ISP for Your Internet Connection

Before you can consider setting up your own server on the Internet, you need the right type of connection. That means *static IP addressing* rather than *dynamically allocated IP addressing*.

IP addresses are the strings of numbers that identify computers on the Internet. Whether you realize it or not, your software has the IP addresses for your ISP, so it knows where to send messages. The ISP has an IP address for your dial-up connection so it can return the messages. When you use a browser, it sends your current IP address so you can receive Web pages.

With dynamically allocated IP addresses, your ISP gives you a temporary IP address. The next time you dial in, you get a different IP address.

While you can run a Web server this way, there's no way for anyone to know where to find your site. That's why you want a static address. With a static address, you have a location on the Web that anyone will be able to find. Here are some things to consider:

You want a permanent connection to the Internet, not a dial-up that has to be renewed. Your choices are

- ◆ ISDN
- ◆ Cable
- ◆ DSL

Although many businesses use ISDN, it can get expensive with per minute charges if your site is up 24 hours a day. Even if you don't generate a lot of traffic, which keeps down the phone-company charges, ISPs will probably charge for such a service at a premium.

Far better choices, however, are cable Internet and DSL. These are permanent connections, so there is no dialing in and no timed charges. Unfortunately, having a permanent connection is not the same as static IP addresses. Some telephone companies, for example, offer static IP on DSL lines. Others are moving to dynamic IP. It may be that the latter would offer static IP with premium pricing. Check with your provider about these details.

When your ISP and service is set, be sure to ask the ISP for the IP addresses and names for the primary and secondary servers. You need this information to get your domain name.

Apply for Your Domain Name

Now that you have a permanent connection, you need a domain name, such as yourname.com. First, be creative and come up with a domain name that you like and that is not hard to remember. Have a few different possibilities, because you may find that your first—or even second or third—choice is already in use. You will also have three different choices for endings:

- ◆ .com
- ◆ .org
- ◆ .net

Com is typically used for businesses or Web sites put up for private use. Org in the past has indicated a nonprofit organization, though that classification is hardly policed and an ".org" at the end of a domain certainly is no guarantee about what the domain's owner does. The ".net" once meant that the domain was connected directly to the Internet's backbone and not through an ISP. But that is no longer the case, and you should feel free to use yourname.net.

Next, you need to apply for the domain name, pay for it, and start using it. Here are the steps to getting a domain name:

1. Use a browser, and go to Network Solutions (www.networksolutions.com). This company can register new domain names.

2. Enter your first choice of domain name, choose which ending you want to have, and click on Go.

3. If your choice is available, the site will tell you. You will also learn if the name is already registered, but the site will also inform you of any open variations, like the same domain name using the ".net" extension instead of the ".com" extension.

4. When you find an available address to your liking, click on Continue. You have the choice to reserve or register the name. Reserving the name is like keeping it on hold. Registering, which is cheaper, is only possible if you already have an IP address.

5. If you choose to register, you will be prompted for the server name(s) and IP address(es) from your ISP.

6. In either case, you will get a series of screens prompting you for the necessary contact and billing information.

Once you are through with the process, you have your own domain name.

Prepare a Server

When it comes to having an Internet server, peer-to-peer networking just won't do. You need a client/server network operating system. Although there are a number of choices on the market, the best is undoubtedly Linux.

Commercial releases of Linux are inexpensive, yet bring all the power of a Unix system to bear. With the power comes some complexity, too much for the scope of this book.

A good reference for setting up your own Linux server is *Mastering Linux Premium Edition,* by Arman Danesh (Sybex, 1999). It contains all the information you need to create and manage your own Linux server, and it comes with a copy of the operating system itself.

39 Run Your Own E-mail System

It is a pain to be limited to one e-mail address and expensive to maintain more. With a network, though, there's no need for this limitation. You can create as many e-mail addresses as you need. There are two ways you can go about this: manage your own e-mail server, or use a proxy mail server.

Manage Your Own E-mail Server

You can set up your own e-mail server if you have put a Linux Internet host on your network. (See "38. Connect Your Network to the Internet.") Although beyond the scope of this book, you can find directions on how to set up an e-mail server on a Linux computer in *Mastering Linux Premium Edition,* by Arman Danesh (Sybex, 1999).

Use Proxy E-mail

Even if you don't want to run your own Internet host, there is actually a way to make your e-mail account do double—or triple, or quadruple, or even more—duty while saving money. Just use proxy e-mail.

With proxy e-mail, a program effectively becomes an e-mail server for all the network users by acting as an intermediary between them and a single e-mail account. People can send e-mail and the proxy software will send it through the e-mail account on the ISP.

The proxy software uses a single e-mail address but combines it with each user's name, like this:

```
Marty Anderson <ouraccount@isp.com>
```

The e-mail account with the brackets is used by the Internet while leaving the person's name at the front. When the proxy application reads the address, it notes the person's name and sends the e-mail to the appropriate PC.

Wizmail from Lovdahl Consulting—the same company that makes the Webetc proxy server for sharing an Internet connection—is an e-mail proxy. By installing it on your network, you can run your entire e-mail system with a single e-mail account on your ISP.

40 Create Your Own Web Server

If you ever wanted your own Web site, your choice has been to get space on an ISP's server. But why not host a Web site yourself? Here are some of the things you can run on it:

◆ Personal Web pages

◆ A site for your own business

◆ E-commerce

Creating a server that will run directly on the Internet requires a few things:

◆ An ISP account with static IP addresses

◆ A proper server, such as a PC running Linux

◆ A firewall, which can be run on the Linux box

◆ Web server software, such as Apache

This is too complicated for the scope of this book. You can learn more about creating a full-featured Web server intended for open use on the Internet in the book, *Mastering Linux Premium Edition,* by Arman Danesh (Sybex, 1999).

What isn't nearly so complicated, though, is creating your own intranet server. Many people don't realize that Windows 98 comes with the Personal Web Server, or PWS. This is a server intended for low volume Web use. It can let you create an Internet in your home. It doesn't have the power or security to run openly on the Internet, but it is fine to do things such as:

◆ Displaying household schedules and chore lists

◆ Testing your regular Web site before it goes live

◆ Designing a science project for children

PWS will help you set up a Web site, create a personal home page, and allow you to drag-and-drop documents to publish them.

Installing PWS is different from installing other parts of Windows. You need to follow these steps:

1. Click Start ➢ Settings ➢ Control Panel. Double-click Add/Remove Programs.

2. Click the Install button, and insert your Windows 98 CD into a file server on the network. If a Windows 98 program automatically starts, exit out of it. Then click Next.

3. Click the Browse button. Double-click the Add-Ons folder and then the PWS folder. Highlight `setup.exe`, and click Open.

4. Click Finish. You will get the Personal Web Server installation screen. Click Next, and then click Typical.

5. Click Next. When the installation is done, you will see a screen with a Finish button. Click it.

6. Before you can really use the PWS, you will have to restart the computer.

You can now start experimenting with creating Web sites and applications on your home network. For information on how to use PWS, select Start ➢ Programs ➢ Microsoft Personal Web Server ➢ Product Documentation. Look through the topics on the left side of the browser for more information on how to use PWS.

41 Protect Your Kids on the Internet

If you think stories about the dangers to kids on the Internet are media hype, think again. There are many dangers online for children, including:

◆ Sick individuals (pedophiles) with unhealthy sexual and psychological involvement with children

◆ Internet sites about sex

◆ Gambling sites

- People spreading hate literature and philosophies
- A constant barrage of advertising

For those reasons, a computer is a poor babysitter, according to Dr. Joseph Katz, professor emeritus at the University of South Carolina, who has run the education areas for CompuServe and MSN. He likens using the Internet to seeing a villian on TV who can actually reach out, grab your children, and empty your bank account. Yet there are some sensible steps you can take to minimize the danger:

- Monitor what your kids are doing. Problems occur precipitously when children go online completely unsupervised.

- Don't let children go online while behind closed doors. Put the computer the kids use in an open area, such as a playroom or den. If something troubling is going on, there's more of a chance you will see it.

- When watching the kids on the computer, actually watch the screen. Don't assume because you are in the same room that you will know if trouble is brewing.

- Know with whom the children correspond. Because the Internet is such an anonymous medium, you cannot tell for sure who is behind an e-mail address. Keep tabs on whom they talk to.

- Find kid-friendly areas. While problems are always possible, it's much safer if you use a service where adults acknowledge the problems exist and are concerned about them.

- If kids want to chat, insist they use monitored chat rooms. These are chat areas with staff members who watch what happens and who can eject unscrupulous characters. Be careful, though, because some services may offer both monitored and nonmonitored chat rooms, and monitors cannot necessarily see private messages sent from one user to another.

- Reams of unpleasant material is sent via junk e-mail. Although there are features in e-mail programs to filter out adult content, they miss a lot. Have e-mail for your kids go to your e-mail account where you can review it and pass on to them only what you deem acceptable.

There is also software that can help in keeping your kids safe. One type is *filtering* software. Such programs use databases of sites known for adult content, gambling, and hate literature as well as keyword identification. They prevent these by keeping browsers from reaching those sites. Because there is the possibility that filtering software might block out a legitimate site—for example, a medical site with information about sexually transmitted diseases—there is typically a password mechanism to bypass the protection.

Use Filtering Software on Your PCs

One example of filtering software is CYBERsitter, an evaluation copy of which is available online. Here's how to install it:

1. Point a browser to www.cybersitter.com, and download the evaluation version of the product to each PC. Remember that a computer left unprotected is one that kids will use.

2. Find the file on your hard drive, and double-click it.

3. Follow the installation routine.

4. When asked to reboot your computer, click Yes.

Click Start ➤ Program ➤ CYBERsitter ➤ CYBERsitter. You will see the following screen:

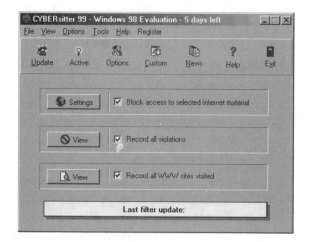

Because the sites with adult content are constantly changing, you need to periodically update the CYBERsitter files. You do this by clicking the Update icon.

No software is perfect, and kids are ingenious when it comes to getting around the limitations of technology, which is why you should also consider a product to examine what children have been looking at. One such product is One Tough Computer Cop from Computer Concepts Corporation. You can review what your kids have been looking at online. It doesn't install onto a computer but runs directly from a CD-ROM drive. That may seem like an inconvenience, but it prevents anyone from tampering with the software.

Enable Internet Explorer's Content Advisor

You can also instruct Internet Explorer to filter sites based on their content. IE has a feature called Content Advisor that uses a volunteer rating system from the Recreational Software Advisory Council on the Internet (RSACi). Under the RSACi, sites can rate themselves on a scale of zero to four for language, violence, sex, and nudity.

You can configure Content Advisor to prohibit the display of sites that score above a particular rating. For example, if you restricted language to 0, or inoffensive slang, then a site with any higher rating would be unavailable.

Here's how to set up Content Advisor:

1. Select Internet Options from the View menu.

2. Select the Content tab.

3. Click Enable under Content Advisor.

4. Provide a password that will be necessary to change Content Advisor settings or to turn it off. Click OK.

5. Select each of the criteria, and decide what level you wish to permit.

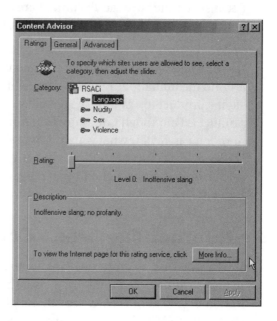

6. Select the General tab, and ensure that Users Can See Sites That Have No Rating is not selected, which means unrated sites will not be visible. Now you have another mechanism in place to keep children from finding themselves in inappropriate places.

42 Set Up Your Own Private "Neighborhood" Network

It's great to have neighbors, not only when you see them on the street but when you meet them on the information superhighway. You may find some you want to invite into your home—electronically, that is. By creating a dial-up server, you can let other people use your network. (See "22. Remotely Access Your Home Network with a Windows 98 Dial-Up Server.")

With an Internet host and a full Web server, you might even let them come in from the Internet.

There are many things you can do when neighbors have access, such as

◆ Let neighborhood kids work together on schoolwork.

◆ Share cooking recipes.

◆ Play computer games with others without leaving the house.

There are a few things to remember. One is to set up security on your network. If you have private information, put it all together on a hard drive, and make it unavailable.

Also, be sure to set up passwords so not everyone can dial up. If you run a Linux server, you can even look to creating user-level access, instead of share level, to provide a greater level of control.

```
************
KUDZU BOOKS
CHAMBLEE
THANK YOU
770-458-9277

NO CASH REFUNDS
ALL SALES FINAL
Exchanges With Receipt
Within 10 Days
Have A Nice Day !
08-16-2003  12:17   1001
REG   Kim        000029


Computer      T₁      $6.99
TL                    $7.48
TA1                   $6.99
TX1                   $0.49
CH                    $7.48
```

Use Your Network to Communicate with the World

The convenience of keeping files and applications on servers can make you forget the many other things you can do with a network. Let's talk, for a change, about talking—and phoning and faxing and even sending messages to people in your home and anywhere else in the world. Look at some of the things you can do with your network:

♦ Use your Internet connection to make inexpensive phone calls.

♦ Add video phoning to your communications choices.

♦ Add faxing to your home repertoire with a fax server.

♦ Run a full-featured answering system for your phone.

♦ Let your network run a home intercom system.

♦ Add voice to your e-mail.

Not only does your network provide data communications but it can help meet all of your telecommunications needs while saving you money. Instead of adding phone lines, just use your computer to better manage the ones you already have.

43 Turn Your Network into an Internet Phone Exchange

Once you have a connection to your ISP from your home network, you can leverage the power of data communications to make phone calls around the world and, in the process, save money.

In fact, if you are trying to reach someone else who has an Internet connection, you can make that phone call for practically nothing. All you need are

♦ A connection from your network to your ISP

♦ Sound cards on the PCs

♦ Microphones

♦ Speakers or ear phones

♦ Special IP telephony software

One communication technique is called *IP telephony,* or voice-over IP. Communication over the Internet works by taking information you want to send, breaking it up into pieces called *packets,* and transmitting it from one computer on the Internet to the next until the packets reach their final destination. Then the recipient's computer reassembles the packets.

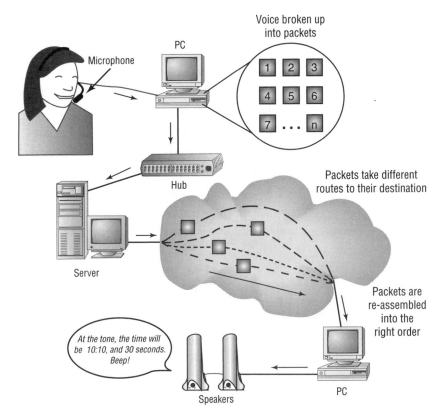

By plugging in a microphone, your sound card turns your voice into digital information that can travel via an IP connection. The PC on the other end of the conversation reassembles the packets into the sound of your voice. Similarly, anything said by the other party travels to your computer, where it plays over your speakers or earphones.

The biggest drawback to how this works is *latency,* or delay, which means that like everything else on the Internet, voices have to take their turns. So don't be thrown if there's a delay between when you say something and when someone hears it. In the time gaps, think of the money you aren't paying to a long-distance phone company.

Make IP Telephony Calls in NetMeeting

Although your network may be ready to provide the Internet connection, you still need to configure each PC that will act as a phone. The first step is making sure your hardware is ready:

1. You need a sound card on the PC. If necessary, purchase one, and install it according to the manufacturer's instructions. Make sure you get a 16-bit or a 32-bit sound card, not an 8-bit card, so you aren't limited in capabilities.

2. Plug in a microphone. Some computers have built-in microphones, but you may find that an external microphone closer to your mouth works better.

3. Plug in speakers or earphones. Earphones are probably better, because they isolate what you hear from the microphone, which could lead to echoes and even feedback screeches.

NOTE A great, comfortable solution to using earphones and having a microphone near you is wearing a headset that has a boom mike that comes off an earpiece and sits near your mouth. I use one made by GN Netcom.

With the PCs set to record and play sound, the next stage is to install software that handles voice-over IP. There are a number of choices on the market, many of which require the other party to use the same software. One quick answer to this is to choose something free and ubiquitous.

Microsoft NetMeeting is an Internet phone program available for download (www.microsoft.com/NetMeeting). You can use NetMeeting if a PC runs Windows 95, 98, or NT. NetMeeting also comes with Windows 98. If you don't have NetMeeting, go to the Microsoft site and follow the directions.

Configure NetMeeting

Once NetMeeting is in place, you have to configure it, which happens automatically when you use it for the first time:

1. Click Start ➤ Programs ➤ Internet Explorer ➤ Microsoft NetMeeting.

2. Click Next. You can log onto a public directory server that lists people who are interested in chatting. If you don't want to automatically log onto a directory server, deselect the choice. You can always log onto a server later. Click Next.

3. You have to provide a first name, last name, and e-mail address to use NetMeeting. However, there is no prohibition against using an initial for either name.

4. When you are logged into a directory server, NetMeeting will indicate your general interest. Click one of the choices, and then click Next.

5. Indicate the type of connection you will use, and then click Next.

6. The Audio Tuning wizard will start. You can also start it by choosing Audio Tuning Wizard from the Tools menu on NetMeeting.

7. Be sure the volume on your earphones or speakers is at an acceptable level, and then click Next.

8. Press Test and adjust the slider until you can hear the sound the wizard plays, and then click Next.

9. Read the text displayed on the screen, and adjust the recording level slider control so, as you speak, you see green sound levels that periodically move into yellow. If you see red displayed, turn down the recording level.

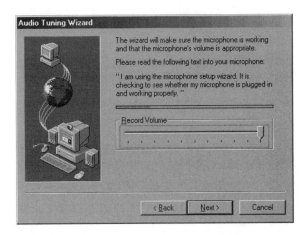

10. Click Next and then Finish.

Once you have set the levels, you will see the NetMeeting window. Now you are ready to place a call.

Place a Call through a NetMeeting Server

There are two ways of establishing a call to someone. The first is for both parties to log onto a NetMeeting server to speak over the Internet.

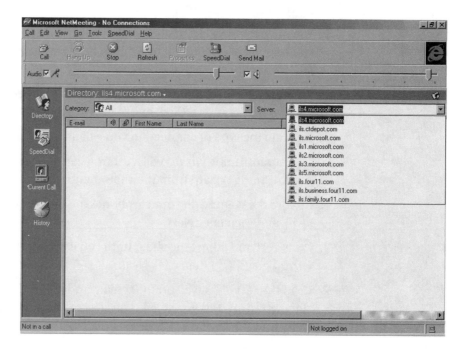

There are a number of sources for servers to use. Microsoft has six different servers, named ils.microsoft.com, ils1.microsoft.com, ils2.microsoft .com, and so on, through ils5.microsoft.com. The Microsoft servers are often busy, so you may want to look at some alternatives:

◆ CTDepot.com has a server, ils.ctdepot.com, as well as extensive information on IP telephony.

◆ Four11.com (ils.four11.com) has a few servers, one rated for family chat and another for business use.

◆ The NetMeeting Zone (`www.netmeet.net`) has lists of servers as well as resources for NetMeeting users.

Though you and the other party can log onto different servers, it's easiest when you are both on the same server. Here's how you place a call:

1. Make arrangements, perhaps via e-mail, with the other party to log onto a directory server and decide who will initiate the call.

2. Start NetMeeting by clicking Start ➢ Programs ➢ Internet Explorer ➢ Microsoft NetMeeting.

3. Click the Call icon.

4. If you are initiating the call, type in the other person's e-mail address, and wait for the other party to accept a conversation.

5. If the other party is initiating the call, accept the call when you receive the notice in NetMeeting.

You can now talk with the other party as long as your voices—and Internet connections—hold out.

Place a Call through ICQ

You can avoid going through a server altogether by using ICQ. This popular, free Internet chat program has an option that can connect you in a NetMeeting session to another user of the program. Because you can keep a list of contacts and receive notification when they are online, it is much easier to arrange a call.

You will need the special version of ICQ that supports NetMeeting. Go to www.icq.com, and follow the directions for downloading and installing the program. You also need to install an additional program, ICQ for Net-Meeting. Once in place, here's how to start a NetMeeting session:

1. Look for the person you wish to speak with on your ICQ contact list.

2. Highlight the name.

3. Left-click and choose Microsoft NetMeeting.

4. Enter a subject if you want, and then click Send.

When your request is accepted, ICQ will start NetMeeting and you can begin your conversation.

44 Call a Regular Telephone with an IP Telephony Service

Besides making phone calls from your network to a PC on the Internet, you can also use IP telephony to reach a regular telephone practically anywhere in the world!

To do this, you need to use a service that can take the call at the receiving end and place it over a local phone line near the recipient.

NOTE This type of call can make economic sense, but it depends on the location you want to reach and what the normal long-distance charges might be. Within North America, for example, it's easy to find long-distance services that are less expensive. If you are calling overseas, however, you will have to search to find some bargain rates.

To place a call from your network to a regular computer, you first have to choose a service provider. Some, such as Deltathree.com (www.deltathree .com), have their own IP networks for better call characteristics of clarity and decreased latency, though high-quality calls probably end when you cross international boundaries. Here are the steps you need to take:

1. Pick a service provider, and set up an account.

2. Download from the service provider whatever special software you need to use the service.

3. Pay money into your account via credit card, wire transfer, or check, depending on the provider's policies.

4. To actually make the call, dial it with the downloaded software, and then use your microphone and earphones or speakers as you would for a regular IP telephone call.

You should then be able to call who you wish.

WARNING To complete a call, the other party has to be within an area that the IP telephony company can reach by a local call from its presence in the region. You may not be able to reach persons outside major metropolitan areas.

45

Manage Phone Calls when Your Network Dials Up the Internet

It's altogether too easy to miss important phone calls when using the Internet, especially when your network dials out on a regular telephone line. But even some types of high-speed Internet connections can leave you at the mercy of your own busy signal. Using both channels on an ISDN line, for instance, makes it unable to accept a phone call. This can be aggravating when someone else on the network gets on the Internet, sometimes without your knowing.

There are a few strategies you can use to avoid playing an elongated round of busy signals:

♦ Install particular broadband technologies.

♦ Make use of the telephone features available in most areas.

♦ Use Internet call-management services.

Even if you can't take a phone call when it comes in, you will at least know whose calls you missed.

Get Your Calls with Broadband Technology

The obvious problem with a regular telephone line is that it's only one line. By using broadband Internet connections, though, you might as well free up the line for talk.

A cable connection would seem like the obvious choice, but only if it's two-directional cable. If it's one directional, then you will need a regular phone line to transmit files or your commands.

DSL is a good solution, because the data carried over DSL runs at a much higher electrical frequency than voice traffic. That means you can receive a telephone call while you are connected to the Internet.

Satellite service might sound suitable, but again you need to use a regular phone line to send commands and files, so it's no better than one-way cable.

Use Standard Telephone Features

There are two phone features available in most areas that can help avoid problems with missing phone calls. One is call answering. The telephone company acts as your answering service. If your network is using the phone line to dial up an ISP, people telephoning you will immediately find themselves in your voice-mail system. In some areas, there is also an option of multiple voice mailboxes, so everyone at home can receive private messages.

WARNING There is always a little doubt as to whether you receive all your messages. I use call answering on the phone lines in my home, and I've periodically found messages not showing up until days after they were left.

Call forwarding is another good feature. You set your phone to forward incoming calls to another number, such as a cell phone, *before* your network dials the ISP. Because it doesn't affect outgoing communications, your network can call as it needs to. Calls coming into that phone, on the other hand, are redirected to the number you specified.

Beware of the call-waiting feature, though. The tone you hear indicating another call disrupts a modem connection. In fact, dial-up networking in Windows gives you the option of disabling call waiting for that very reason.

WARNING If you have both call waiting and call answering, disabling the former for an outgoing call also can disable the latter, so people telephoning will receive a busy signal.

Use Internet Call Management Services

A third approach is to use Internet call-management services, in which a company lets you know who is calling while you are online. One of the

Internet call-management services is Internet Call Manager (www
.internetcallmanager.com). Here's how it works:

1. You forward your phone to a number designated by the service
   provider.

2. When a call comes in, the service provider identifies the caller with a
   Caller ID and then informs the person to hold.

3. The service provider sends a message over the Internet to software it
   gives you. That software displays the phone number and name of the
   person calling.

4. You have a choice of ignoring the call, telling the person you will call
   back, or asking the other party to call you back.

5. The service provider relays this message to the person.

Although this doesn't let you receive the phone calls as they come in, at
least you know who called and how to reach them.

46 Put a Face Behind the Words with Video Phoning

Hearing a voice over the Internet is fine, but you can also add live video to
your network-based calls, which will let you

◆ Look other people in the eye while doing business.

◆ See as well as hear friends who are far away.

◆ Keep better tabs on kids while they are away at college.

There are a couple of ways you can go about this. You can have one conversation at a time, or you can actually get multiple people on a screen at the
same time. Before making any calls, though, you need some hardware
additions to the PCs on your network.

Install a Video Camera and Board

Video phoning loses some panache without the video. You need to add both a video camera and a frame capture board if your PC is to broadcast images of your smiling face all over creation.

If you've made your PCs ready for television (see "27. Turn Your Networked Computers into Entertainment Stations"), the TV tuner card has frame capture, and you are set. Otherwise, you will have to buy a frame capture board. The best way to find one may be to purchase a package of a board and a small video camera to sit atop the monitor. A number of hardware vendors offer this, or you can purchase a videoconferencing package, such as White Pine's CU-SeeMe, that comes with the necessary hardware.

To install the frame capture board and video camera, use the following general steps:

1. Turn off the PC, unplug it, and open the case.

2. Find a free slot—probably PCI—and insert the board.

3. Close the case, plug in the unit, and start it.

4. Follow the vendor's installation guide. After you are done, turn off the computer again.

5. Take the cord from the video camera and plug it into the video input of the frame capture card.

6. Start the PC again, and plug in the video camera's power supply.

The video teleconference software you choose can now use the hardware to establish a connection.

Make a Single Connection Video Call with NetMeeting

If you want to make a video connection with one other person, NetMeeting is a good choice. Once you ready the computer for IP telephone calls, adding video is easy. Here are the steps you need:

1. Click Start ➢ Programs ➢ Internet Explorer ➢ Microsoft NetMeeting.

2. Under the Tools menu, select Options.

3. Select the Video tab.

4. Choose the video camera source under The Video Capture Device I Wish to Use Is.

5. Choose the small, medium, or large video size. The smaller the picture, the faster and more smoothly video will run.

6. Under Video Quality, move the slider to get the balance between the speed and quality of the received video. Again, the faster the image, which means the more lifelike, the poorer the quality.

NOTE Videoconferencing benefits from faster Internet connections.

7. The Source button may or may not be available, depending on the video capture card.

8. Check both Automatically Send Video at the Start of Each Call and Automatically Receive Video at the Start of Each Call.

Now you can start and run NetMeeting sessions as you do with a strictly audio session.

Make a Multiple Connection Video Call with CU-SeeMe

Here are some reasons you may want more than one person in the same video call:

♦ The family at home can all participate in a call to a college student away from home.

♦ Friends from around the country can see and talk with each other without traveling from their homes.

♦ You need multiple participants in a business conference call.

Microsoft NetMeeting unfortunately cannot accommodate a videoconference-type call, but there is a product called CU-SeeMe that can let you see multiple conference participants at the same time.

WARNING As the number of people videoconferencing increases, the video quality decreases. The higher Internet speed connection your network has, the better you will see the other people.

The original CU-SeeMe was developed at Cornell University and can be found on the CD accompanying this book. To install it, follow these steps:

1. Point a browser to www.cu-seeme.net, and download a copy of the free software. Save it to an empty directory on the hard drive of each networked PC that will use videoconferencing.

2. Use Windows Explorer to find the file.

3. Double-click the file. It will create the file cu-seeme.exe. You can now delete cuseemev10.exe from the hard drive.

For information on how to use the product, see the Cornell Web site (cu-seeme.cornell.edu), which has a user's manual.

Similar to NetMeeting, you can use a server to set up a video connection. In the CU-SeeMe world, it's called a *reflector*—basically a videoconferencing chat room. You can find lists of reflectors, as well as other CU-SeeMe information, at Rocketcharged.com's CU-SeeMe Cool Site (www.rocketcharged .com/cu-seeme). There is also a database of reflectors at the CU-SeeMe Network (www.cu-seeme.net). Click on the Web Reflector Scanner link.

To log onto a reflector follow these steps:

1. Start CU-SeeMe.

2. Under the Conference menu, check Phone Book.

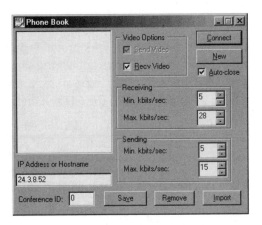

3. Enter the IP address of the reflector you want to use.

4. Click Connect.

You can now converse with people also logged onto the reflector. Two people can also set up a direct connection when they know each other's IP addresses. Chances are that your ISP uses dynamically allocated IP addresses, so it changes each time you log on. Rocketcharged.com has a Java program that will display your IP address (www.rocketcharged.com/cu-seeme/yourip.html). You can also see your IP by using winipcfg. (See "16. Check TCP/IP Performance with Ping and Winipcfg.")

NOTE White Pine Software has a commercial version of CU-SeeMe (www.wpine.com) that has the multiconversion feature with full documentation and technical support.

47 Put an Answering Service on Your Network with Call Center

Not only can your network provide you with Internet telephoning but it can also run a complete answering service for your entire home. To have a network phone answering system, you can use the Call Center shareware from V3, Inc. found on the CD accompanying this book.

To run Call Center, you need a voice modem that will work with this software. See www.v3inc.com for a list of compatible modems. If yours is not, you can find a compatible model for as little as $30.

You can install Call Center with the following steps:

1. Install the program with the user interface on the CD accompanying this book, or install manually by double-clicking the file cc 031899.exe in the directory \Network Communication\Call Center\ on the CD.

2. Click Next twice. You need to provide information, such as a name and a company name, that will be used for fax cover sheets. You might consider using the name "Fax Server" and the company name "Our Household." Then click Next again.

3. Fill in address information to go on fax pages, and then click Next.

4. Add phone number information, and then click Next.

5. Enter the international access number and your country code, and then click Next.

6. Enter your area code and then the number you need for long distance, typically "1." Some business phone systems might require you to enter a digit before dialing local or long-distance numbers. Because most home phone lines don't need this, you will probably leave the fields blank. Then click Next.

7. If you like, add CompuServe and e-mail addresses to put on faxes. Click Next.

8. Leave all three components checked. Be sure the directories listed are networked directories and all the other PCs have full access to them. If not, either change the directories or change their access. Note the names of the directories, as you need the information later. Click Next.

9. Rename the system mailbox if you want, and then click Next.

10. Click Next twice.

11. You can let the program automatically detect your modem port or manually select it. To auto-detect it, click Detect.

12. You may have to select the model of modem. If so, follow the directions on the screen.

13. Click OK.

Now that the software is installed on the server, you can record phone calls. Click Start ➤ Programs ➤ COMponents ➤ Call Center on the server. You will see a screen like the one shown next.

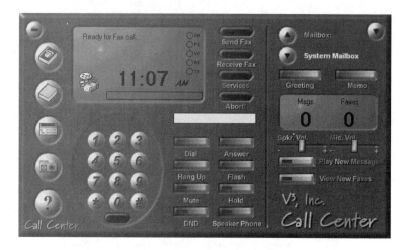

For more convenience, install the software on the other PCs, too. First, install the software to enable full modem sharing and not just the proxy service. (See "12. Share Devices across the Network.") Then install Call Center on all the other PCs, too. When you get to step 9, change the directories to the mapped equivalents of the ones you used when installing the server.

Now you should be able to use Call Center on all of your PCs to check voice mail. Because voice mail is stored in a WAV format, you can also play it with the Media Player that comes with Windows.

The free version of the software on this CD allows only one voice mailbox. By upgrading, you can create individual mailboxes and add more advanced features.

48 Set up a Fax Server

If you ever have to receive faxes at home, there is nothing more convenient than having a fax server. Instead of walking over to the fax machine to pick up piles of paper, you check the fax mailbox on the network server from wherever you are. If you need to send a fax from a program, just use the fax server. All this happens without additional phone lines or modems.

There are various programs available to create a network fax server. Call Center can provide a faxing service. Pressing the send fax button brings up a wizard that walks you through the fax sending process.

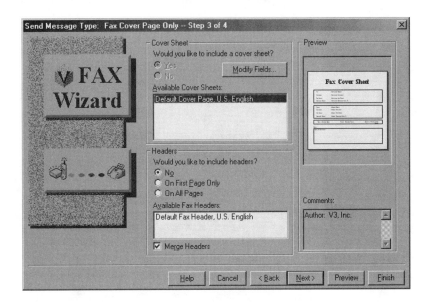

If you run a business out of your home, you might want to consider a package aimed more at network faxing. FaxMail Network for Windows from ElectraSoft is a shareware program that can run on any Windows computer on your network. Because it runs in the background, the program won't interfere with anything else the computer is doing. To install it, use this procedure:

1. Point a browser to www.electrasoft.com. Click on the link to download FaxMail Network for Windows. Save the file fmn.zip to an empty directory on a network file server that has a fax modem.

2. Unarchive the file. You can download an evaluation version of Winzip, which handles archived files in Windows, from www.winzip.com.

3. Find install.exe, and double-click it.

4. Follow the directions in the installation program. You will have to provide a name and phone number for the faxes.

5. Once you have installed the program on the server, install it on your other PCs. The installation program will prompt you for a network drive to use. Give it the correct map letter for each PC.

Click Start ➤ Programs ➤ FaxMail Network for Windows ➤ FaxMail Tutor to learn how to use the system. To start the program, click Start ➤ Programs ➤ FaxMail Network for Windows ➤ FaxMail. This provides the work center for

♦ Sending and viewing faxes

♦ Monitoring activity

♦ Creating cover pages

Now anyone on your network can send and view faxes.

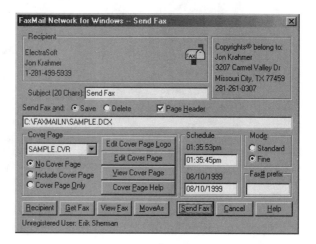

49 Create a Home Intercom System

Shouting from room to room may do a lot to develop good breathing and vocal capacity, but it is hardly necessary when you have a home computer network. Instead add an intercom system to your network.

Use NetMeeting for Messages, Audio, and Video

If you used NetMeeting for IP telephony or video phoning over the Internet, you'll be glad to know that it also works on networks. Your network has to run TCP/IP as one of its protocols. (See "19. Let Computers Talk with a Network Protocol.")

Follow these steps to place a call to someone else on the network:

1. Click Start ➤ Programs ➤ Internet Explorer ➤ Microsoft NetMeeting.

2. Click the Call icon, or press CTRL+N. You will now see the New Call dialog box.

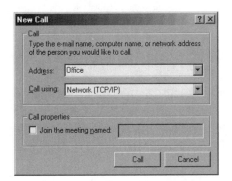

3. Under Call Using, select Network (TCP/IP).

4. Under Address, type in the network name of the PC you want to reach. Then click Call.

The person at the other PC will receive a call request and can either accept to talk or decline if busy. Instead of declining, someone can also use a chat session. After receiving a call, click Chat under the Tools menu. This brings up the chat window so you can send messages back and forth.

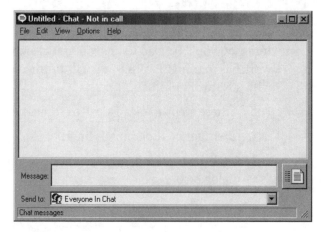

Send a Windows Pop-Up Message

You can also send a quick message to someone on your network with Win-Popup, a program that comes with Windows. While running, WinPopup lets you and other users send and receive messages. To load WinPopup, follow these steps:

1. Right-click Start, and then select Find.

2. Type winpopup.exe in the space next to Named.

3. Click Browse.

4. Highlight [C:], and click OK.

5. Check Include subfolders.

6. Click Find Now.

7. Double-click on the WinPopup application.

8. If the system cannot find WinPopup, then click Start ➢ Settings ➢ Control Panel. Double-click on Add/Remove Programs.

9. Select the Windows Setup tab.

10. Highlight System Tools, and click Details.

11. Check WinPopup, and click OK twice.

12. Follow steps one through seven.

With these steps, you have loaded WinPopup and are ready to send and receive messages over your network.

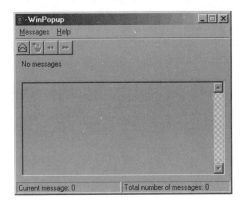

Choose how you want WinPopup to run as follows:

1. Under the Messages menu, choose Options.

2. Check whether you want to hear a sound when messages arrive, whether WinPopup stays at the front of your screen, and whether WinPopup pops up when a message arrives.

3. Click OK.

WinPopup will now behave the way you configured it. To send a message when WinPopup is active, either select Send from the Messages menu or press CTRL+S.

You can also have WinPopup start every time you turn on your PC by adding it to the Startup group:

1. Click Start ➢ Settings ➢ Taskbar&Start Menu.

2. Select the Start Menu Programs tab.

3. Click Add.

4. Type **C:\Windows\Winpopup.exe**, where *C:* is the drive with the Windows directory on it.

5. Click Next.

6. Highlight StartUp, and click Next.

7. Call the shortcut WinStartup, and then click Finish.

Now every time your system starts, WinPopup will be ready to connect you to everyone else on your network with a simple message system.

Support Your Home Office with Your Home Network

Until the unlikely day a prize van drives to your home with a check for $10,000,000, don't plan to ban mentions of work in your home. However, with your own network, you can make the intrusion—whether bringing work back from the office or running a business from your home—more profitable. Here are some of the things you can do:

♦ "Meet" with clients through video teleconferencing and stop wasting time traveling.

♦ Connect your network to your office.

♦ Run an e-business from home.

♦ Offer a fax information system.

♦ Run contact information systems that rival sophisticated corporate software.

♦ Do market research.

♦ Learn about your customers with e-surveys.

♦ Project the impression of a larger company.

♦ Enable a virtual company through online collaboration.

Because you have a home network, you can offer all these services without unduly burdening a single computer system.

50 Put Your "Real" Office on the Other End of Your Network

There is a distinct pleasure in describing your commute as walking from the bedroom to a home office. But even when working outside the home, your network can bring some great advantages:

♦ Work at home to spend less time in meetings and more time in productive activities.

- ◆ Backup important projects to your home network for safety and convenience.

- ◆ Telecommute through your home network into the office.

- ◆ Work in comfortable clothes, and take the odd break without the need to appear busy.

- ◆ If you have a pressing project, go home at a regular hour, and finish it on your network, avoiding a commute when you are tired.

Those who want to try a hand at the new domestic tranquillity will find there have never been so many ways of connecting to work. The first step is to understand which method you will use, after which you need to spend some time getting ready.

Connect to Work

With dial-up communications, the Internet, and even moving a computer back and forth between work and home, there are many ways to connect your work between the office and home.

Talk to your company's network administrator or MIS department, and explain what you want to do—after speaking with your supervisor, of course. Ask about the types of access the company offers, and then work within their restrictions.

Understand what you must do to meet security requirements. This may involve your usual user ID and password or additional codes that you may need to supply upon the demand of the remote-access server.

Many companies are putting security measures into place that might require you to have a *digital certificate* or a special electronic document proving that you are whom you claim to be. If needed, get the details of how to obtain one and install it. In such a case, you will probably be restricted to using one particular PC on your network.

Connect over the Internet

An expanding practice among corporations is to create an *intranet,* or internal network that uses Internet technologies and standards. On one hand, the network may hook into the Internet to allow those outside a physical office access to resources. On the other hand, it is a private network, not available to just anyone. You would be able to use your own network's connection to the Internet and a browser to get to company resources.

To use an intranet, you may need any of the following:

- ◆ A user ID
- ◆ A password
- ◆ A URL for entry
- ◆ Plug-ins for your browser
- ◆ A *smart card,* which provides an access password that keeps changing

See the technical department at your company to learn exactly what you will need as well as any special settings your browser might need.

Dial-Up Work Directly

Just as you can create a dial-up server on your own network, a company may have a *remote-access server* that lets you directly call the office. You will need to get one or more of the following from either the MIS department or network administrator:

- ◆ A user ID
- ◆ A password
- ◆ A *smart card,* which provides an access password that keeps changing
- ◆ A telephone number for the remote access server

If the company does not have a way to dial up, you still may be able to do so. If you have a Windows 98 PC, you can turn it into a dial-up server as explained in "22. Remotely Access Your Home Network with a Windows 98 Dial-Up Server." This will give you access to that machine and might actually put you on the network, especially if you use Traveling Software's LapLink as the remote control software.

WARNING If you choose to go this route, be sure to speak with technical personnel at your company. Many corporate telephone systems are incompatible with regular modems and can damage them. There may also be times that your PC is required to be unused because of network backups. Finally, be wary of leaving a back door of your network open for hackers to use.

Use a Laptop as a Go-Between

When you can't get a direct connection, a laptop can become an electronic dump truck, hauling loads of files from one location to the next. Look at the sections in "Connect to Your Home Network on the Run" that discuss synchronizing a laptop to your home network. You can use the same techniques to use the laptop with the network at your office. The laptop then becomes the indirect mechanism for keeping home and office in sync as follows:

1. Set up synchronization between the laptop and the office desktop.

2. Transfer and update files at the end of the day.

3. When home, set up synchronization between the laptop and a networked PC.

4. Transfer and update files before leaving for work.

You effectively synchronize your office desktop and home network in this fashion.

You can also make a laptop your primary computer at work. With a PC Card NIC, you will be able to connect it directly to the corporate network. If you use the same type of physical network—say 10baseT or 100BaseT—then the single PC Card can do double duty.

NOTE There are some PC Card NICs that support a mix of network technologies, such as a combination of both Ethernet and phone line networking.

Prepare a Work Site on Your Network

Once you know how you will connect to work, you can prepare your own network to operate efficiently as a second office:

1. Set aside a directory on a network server for work-related files. It may save you time in the long run to use the same directory structure you have on your work PC, so there is never a question as to where a file should be.

2. If there is particular software you need for work, obtain copies and install them.

3. You will need a proxy server to connect via the Internet and port sharing for a direct dial-up connection.

Such an approach should help you keep some organization and make the synchronization process between home and work easier. You should also consider restricting access to the directory so no one else can disrupt your progress:

1. Highlight the directory in the server's Windows Explorer.

2. Right-click the directory, and choose Properties.

3. Select the Sharing tab.

4. Select Shared As, otherwise you won't have access from any computer other than the server.

5. Under Access Type, select Depends on Password.

6. Provide different passwords for read only and full access.

By keeping both passwords secret, you can keep anyone else from gaining access to the directory and, therefore, the files within it.

Now you are ready to work from home.

51 Meet Clients and Associates with Video Teleconferencing

If spending time in endless meetings is bad, having to travel to such meetings is worse. You can immediately cut wasted time conferring with clients or consulting with colleagues by videoconferencing.

As "46. Put a Face Behind the Words with Video Phoning" explains, you can set up videoconferencing to work from your home network with the proper video hardware and software.

But you can hardly be casual in your business dealings, which means some considerations particular to the occasion.

Use a High-Speed Internet Connection

Video teleconferencing works by sending audio and video over the Internet back and forth between the two parties, but the quality of what you get over in this context can vary. Of course, television and video recordings have heightened people's expectations with their quality. To achieve that level of excellence requires between 24 and 32 images taken every second. Even with the compression used in computerized video, that's a boatload of data. One thing that can help is a high-bandwidth connection to the Internet, which can move video and audio from your network to the Internet quickly.

However, bandwidth doesn't help when there is traffic congestion on the Internet. Hand in glove with Internet congestion is *latency,* or how quickly your information travels. Low latency—as with regular phone calls— means transmission happens more or less immediately. But the Internet isn't the telephone network, and your video is subject to the whims of other traffic. That means the video may appear jerky or stuttering. There is nothing you can do for this other than decide when your business might suffer from a poor appearance.

Use Fast PC Video Hardware

Though you can't do anything about Internet traffic, you do have control over a networked PC. Video is very demanding of your system. You might designate one PC as your conferencing system with the following considerations:

◆ The video adapter on your PC should be fast. If necessary, upgrade to a graphics accelerator board with plenty of video memory—at least 8MB of video RAM, with more being preferable.

◆ Raw system speed and memory will also speed the video software's operations. Look, if possible, at a fast Pentium with at least 64MB of RAM.

◆ The quality of video you send will be only as good as the camera you use. There are cheap cameras with images that might be acceptable when talking to a friend but not acceptable in business.

Again, how far you go depends on how important the video quality will be to your business.

Create the Right Atmosphere

The greatest evil brought to a home office by video teleconferencing is the need to look good. If you are speaking with clients, appear professional:

◆ Dress for the part. Yes, the ratty bathrobe and fuzzy slippers may be comfortable, but you are opening your home to prying eyes. Because it's business, look the part. You may get away with dressing decently from the waist up if you will remain seated during the call.

◆ Dress the room. Although a network may let you work virtually anywhere in your home, you will want something presentable. If you must work in the equivalent of an untidy home warehouse, put a screen behind you to shield the clutter.

◆ Shed light on the topic. Video cameras are not mechanical rabbits that see in the dark given a sufficient diet of carrots. Light yourself adequately. Experiment with different illumination levels while watching the window of your own video until you find something that works.

By preparing yourself and the network, videoconferencing can become an important part of home-business operation.

52 Create an E-Business and Run It off Your Network

E-commerce has become all the rage and for good reasons:

◆ The cost of running an e-commerce site can be far less than either establishing a store or running a direct marketing campaign through magazine and newspaper ads or catalogs.

◆ You can reach a niche audience through the Web, broadening the reach of an existing business or permitting you to launch a venture that could not find enough customers in your area.

◆ Modifying your product list, prices, and company or product presentation can happen as fast as you wish.

◆ A Web business allows you to get in front of your customers much faster than with traditional marketing means.

◆ Because customers only see what is on the screen, your business can start to compete with larger companies.

You can hire an ISP to host your business Web site and run the e-commerce portion for you, but this can become an expensive proposition.

Instead, you could host your e-commerce site yourself. Certainly it means you have to deal with technical details, issues, and work that a service provider would otherwise take over, but you get more control over the site's operation and cost.

The general steps you take to develop an e-business are

1. Plan the business.

2. Create an e-commerce server.

3. Test the whole system.

4. Go live.

Creating any kind of a business is far from being a cakewalk, but it can be an enjoyable and rewarding challenge.

Plan the Business

The emphasis on an e-business has to be on the *business* and not the *e*. Do some market research—the Web and your network are handy for that too—to ascertain your competition, potential customers, and unfilled market needs that cry out for attention.

Write a business plan. Although no one likes doing it, don't shrug off creating one by saying it's only important if you want funding. The point of a plan is not to impress an investor so much as it is to force yourself to address important issues and problems. For an electronic extension to an existing business, rework your current business plan.

After you have the business plan, write a marketing plan. It should answer the following questions:

- ◆ Will your Web page offer only product information, or do you plan to support ordering and customer service?

- ◆ If taking orders, do you have a merchant account with a bank for accepting credit cards?

- ◆ How do you plan to publicize and promote the existence of the Web site?

- ◆ Does your site differ from that of your competitors? What does it offer that others don't?

- ◆ How will your site convey the reasons for your customers to buy from you, such as price, availability, quality of goods, promotions, and warranties?

Finally, you need an operations plan. One of the most difficult areas in electronic commerce is making it work with the rest of the world. Customer orders for boxes and barrels must migrate from a computer into the warehouse and finally onto shipping labels. This is one case of forgetting the talk about "Internet speed." Know how you are going to keep up your end of the deal with a customer, or run the risk of receiving bad word of mouth—all over the world.

Create an E-Commerce Server

You need a server on the Internet that can manage all the security and ordering issues that belong to e-commerce. A good choice in this case is Linux. Being based on Unix, not only does Linux offer robust security, power, and reliability but it's considerably cheaper than any other choice. Section "38. Connect Your Network to the Internet" discusses many of the issues you have to consider.

NOTE Red Hat, Inc. (www.redhat.com) has a version of Linux called the Red Hat Linux E-Commerce Server, which comes with 128-bit encryption and a variety of e-commerce software.

Test the Whole System

The single biggest headache you could have this year is to let an e-commerce system be available to customers without testing it to excess. Doing so would be the equivalent of opening an entire business—from sales and customer service to billing and inventory—without being sure that any of your business processes worked before you had to use them.

Here are some stages you can use in testing:

1. Test each part of the system as you get it ready. This will help ensure that you detect many problems that might be more elusive when your entire system is running.

2. Run the e-commerce engine internally on your network, and test it there in isolation. Again, by keeping things under your control, you can find errors more easily than if you immediately connected over the Internet.

3. Only when things work on your own network should you make them available to the Internet. Even then, keep the e-commerce URL a secret and continue testing. Be sure that you get the same results.

4. Tired eyes make tired testing. Use people new to the system, including friends and relatives. Also consider hiring some strangers to try placing some orders. They have no vested interest in keeping on your good side.

5. Don't stop with the software. Make sure all of the components of the business work, from updating product descriptions to orders, payment, and shipping. It isn't a good idea to have an e-commerce server smoothly take orders and accept payment if the products languish in a spare bedroom long enough to enrage your customers.

When everything seems to work, then it's time to go live and wish yourself some good fortune. Even if you decide to have an ISP host your e-commerce site, the exercise of ironing out the wrinkles will have incalculable benefits when the process runs as smoothly as possible.

53 Use Fax Systems to Get Information to Your Customers

In business, it sometimes seems that customers are as big a bane as boon. Handling inquiries and support issues can keep you from taking orders. You can use a *fax-on-demand* system—also known as a *fax-back system*—to help keep your attention where you want it. The benefits are extraordinary:

◆ Customers or prospects can hold lengthy information in their hands rather than wading through pages on your Web site.

◆ It's much faster to create formatted fax documents by scanning paper than it is to fuss with HTML.

◆ Someone without access to the Web may have access to a fax machine.

◆ With 24-hour a day availability, you can satisfy customer requests without paying someone to sit by the phones.

In short, you save time and money while customers get what they want when they want it. A good fax system can also help you in gaining business. You can fax price lists, specials, promotions, and other forms of marketing to prospects anywhere in the world.

WARNING If someone asks to be taken off your fax promotion list, do it immediately. Federal law has provisions that can result in fines for those who ignore such requests.

Many fax systems require special hardware. Although handy for high volumes, a home business can often do with less, such as a fax modem. The upgrade of the version of Call Center that you will find on the CD accompanying this book (see "47. Put an Answering Service on Your Network with Call Center") has a built-in fax back system. To configure it, use this procedure:

1. Click Start ➢ Programs ➢ COMponents ➢ Call Center.

2. Click the Display Setting Dialog icon, which is just above the question mark on the left side of Call Center.

3. Select Mailbox Setup.

4. Select the Fax-on-Demand tab.

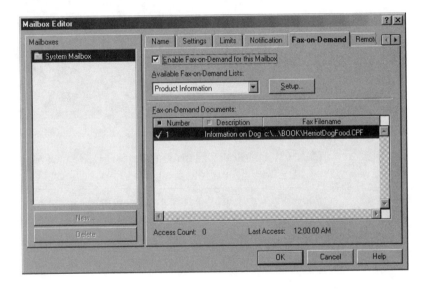

5. Select Enable Fax-on-Demand for this Mailbox.

6. If this is your first fax-on-demand offering, click Setup.

7. Click New, add a new name, and then click OK.

8. Click Add to choose, and add a document to the fax-on-demand list.

NOTE The files you add must be in a fax format. Call Center has a print driver you can use to fax from an application. Use the print driver to create a fax format file of any document you want to send. If you have a paper document, scan the pages in, then open each in an application such as Microsoft Paint, and use the print driver to create the fax files.

9. Assign a document number that customers can use.

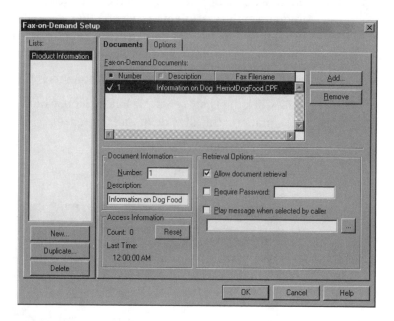

10. Check Allow Document Retrieval. You can require a password to restrict access. Click OK.

People can now dial into your fax number and receive the document. Sending a fax to many people is even easier:

1. Click Start ➤ Programs ➤ COMponents ➤ Call Center.

2. Click the Send Fax button.

3. Follow the directions of the wizard.

4. Either select the individuals or select a group to which you have added the recipients.

5. In the last section of the wizard, you can schedule the day and time for faxing. Set it to a time when your fax line will be open and the server will not be busy backing up the network.

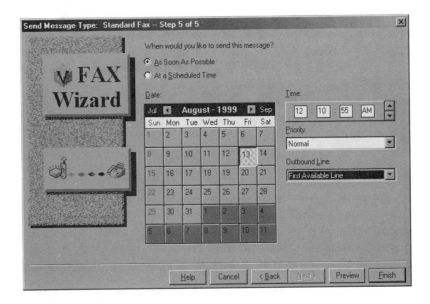

The application will then send the fax at the convenient time you have specified.

54 Make Your Voice Mail Sound Like a Business

One of the telltale signs of a tiny business is a single voice mailbox, recorded by the president, for the entire company. With Call Center, you can create multiple mailboxes for different people or departments on your network and add a professional touch to boot:

1. Start Call Center.

2. Click the Display Settings Dialog.

3. Select Mailbox Setup.

4. Click New to create a new mailbox.

Besides creating a flexible number of voice mailboxes, you might consider hiring a professional to record your voice-mail greetings.

55 Network Your Vital Business Information with Ziata!

Your business can rocket ahead with leading-edge network technology that will put you in control of your data. You can

- ◆ Manage all your business information far more easily than ever before.

- ◆ Reduce data-entry time.

- ◆ Keep track of what your company needs to do.

- ◆ Automatically e-mail customers when necessary.

- ◆ Control relations among contacts, companies, customers, to-do lists, and any other type of information you track.

- ◆ Note telephone messages and know when to interrupt someone.

Ziata! from Ziata Solutions, LLC, gives you powerful and flexible control over your business processes and all your information. Instead of retyping company names, phone numbers, titles, or anything else, you store the basic pieces of information and relate them together.

As with many things that are complex on the surface, the best way to explain how something works is by example. Say you had a company as a customer and dealt with five people at one location. To add new contacts at the same location, you would enter their names and relate them to the company and their particular location. Suddenly all the address information for the new people is the same for the others. Should that location of the company move, you only change the address in one place; the new address now appears in all the contacts.

Each bit of information, an e-mail, or file is an object to Ziata!, which tracks how one object relates to another. Have a deadline for a project? Relate the date to the project—which in turn relates to your customer and everyone working on the project! You can even send automatic reminders by e-mail. As with the example, the best way to understand this powerful program is by using it.

On the CD accompanying this book is a limited time copy of Ziata! that will support up to 100 users. To install it, follow these steps:

1. Install the program with the user interface on the CD accompanying this book, or install manually by double-clicking the file Setup.exe in the directory \Home Office_Home Network\Ziata\ on the CD.

2. Now you need to install and update that adds some enhancements and bug fixes. Install the update with the user interface on the CD accompanying this book, or install manually by double-clicking the file Setup.exe in the directory \Home Office_Home Network\Ziata\ Update on the CD.

3. Click Next, Yes, and then Next.

4. Enter your name and company name, and then click Next twice.

5. Select Yes, Launch the Program File. For some information on the program, also select Yes, I Want to View the README File.

6. Click OK on the Ziata! Profiles window.

7. Select the Basic tab and then Server Installation (Puts Files on Network—Administrator Only). You can change which directory to use if you want.

8. Select the Custom Lists flag. Be sure to select the most appropriate type of industry: legal, software, or generic.

9. Click the Basic tab again, and click OK.

10. Click OK when asked about creating a database.

11. Under the Company Information tab, you have to type the name of your company. Note the spelling, as you will need the same name with exactly the same spelling and capitalization later.

12. Click the right arrows. Enter your name and a password, and then click the right arrows. You will see your nickname. Change it if you want, but you must remember it to log onto the software.

WARNING Be sure to enter the password in the confirmation space, too; otherwise, you will not be able to use the software.

13. Click OK. You will see a screen with your nickname. Highlight it, enter your password, and click OK.

14. When prompted, click Yes twice to back up the data files.

15. Now copy the file update.exe from the CD accompanying this book to an empty directory on the PC. Double-click the file. This updates the program with some modifications and bug fixes.

You can now set up the program for your company. You will see many windows opened up on your screen. These represent many of the different things you can control and track with Ziata!, including

♦ Waiting messages

♦ Staff availability

♦ Deadlines

♦ Automatic generation of deadline notifications

♦ Telephone messages

♦ Surface mail and e-mail

Experiment with the program. The main screen gives you an interface to all parts of the program.

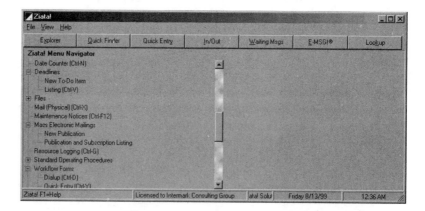

Once everything is set up on the server, you will want to install the program on the other PCs. In the installation process at step 8, choose Workstation Installation instead of Server Installation, and be sure to specify the mapping you will need to reach the Ziata! files residing on your network.

56 Rid Yourself of Paper Piles with a Networked Document Server

The answer to unruly piles of paper threatening to drown you is not a paperweight. Using a home network, you can break through the clutter with a Document Management server. Here are some of the benefits:

♦ Scan pieces of paper and replace them with electronic files.

♦ Combine scanned images, word processing, spreadsheets, and other forms of documents.

♦ Use the keyword search to find what you want.

♦ More than one person can use a document at the same time.

When you combine the convenience with the chance of clearing your desk and saying adieu to filing cabinets, document management could be one of the best things a network can provide.

 On the CD accompanying this book is a free, single-user copy of Optix, an industrial-strength document-management system from Blueridge Technologies, Inc., used by leading corporations. Here's how to install it:

1. For a password to install the product, point a browser to http://www.blueridge.com/osuregistration.html. Fill out the form and you will receive the password via e-mail.

2. Install the program with the user interface on the CD accompanying this book, or install manually by double-clicking the file OPTIX_SUE_540.exe in the directory \Home Office_Home Network\Optix\ on the CD.

3. Click Yes, then enter the password, and click Next.

4. Click Yes to agree to the product license.

5. Read the product information, and click Next twice.

6. Choose a Typical setup, and then click Next three times.

7. Click Finish.

You now have the local file system, workstation module, and user manual in a PDF format. If you don't have the Adobe Acrobat reader, a copy is on the CD accompanying this book. You should note that the manual is for all versions of the product, not just the single-user version, so you may find things that do not apply.

WARNING Always start OPTIX Local Filesystem before OPTIX Workstation.

57 Use Electronic Surveys to Make You Market Smart

Replying to a question about the secret of her success, the star salesperson replied, "I tried asking customers what they wanted first, and then I sold it to them."

It's much easier to have a successful business when you find out what people—whether customers, suppliers, or employees—are actually thinking. It can be expensive to run a telephone or mail survey. With e-mail and the Web, administering surveys becomes easy, cheap, and effective.

The first step is to get some software to help you. On the CD accompanying this book, there are two products from Perseus Development Corporation. One is SurveySolutions Express, a free program that lets you ask a question of visitors to your Web site. The other is SurveySolutions for the Web, which is a limited-time evaluation product that lets you undertake full-featured survey work either from a Web site or via e-mail.

To install the programs, use this procedure:

1. Install the program with the user interface on the CD accompanying this book, or install manually by double-clicking the file setupssxssftw .exe in the directory \Home Office_Home Network\SurveySolutions\ on the CD.

2. Click Next, and then I Agree.

3. You must supply at least your name. You can also optionally provide your company name. Click Next.

4. Specify a location on your file server for the programs. Be sure to use the same location for each PC, even though the mapped drive letter may be different. Click Next twice.

5. The programs will install themselves. SurveySolutions Express will automatically start. You can use it now, or you can close it. To open it later, click Start ➤ Programs ➤ Perseus Applications ➤ Perseus SurveySolutions Express.

You can check the Help menu for information on how to use the product or simply start filling in the blanks and follow the instructions to the right of the screen.

Use SurveySolutions Express

Creating a one-question poll for your Web site is easy with SurveySolutions Express. For example, let's poll people about whether they think their computers will start in the year 2001, which we will dub the Y2K+1 Poll. The following screen shot shows where we've filled in the data.

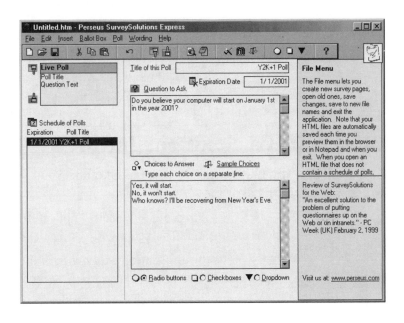

Next, we'll preview the results:

1. Choose Preview in Browser from the Ballot Box menu.

2. Select the browser you want to use for the preview, and click OK.

3. When asked which question to test, enter 1, if not already entered, and press OK. The poll will now appear in the browser.

You can save the survey as an HTML file or even open an existing HTML file to add a survey to what is already stored.

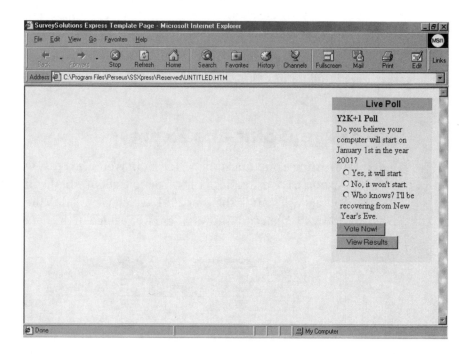

Using SurveySolutions for the Web

SurveySolutions for the Web has far more extensive capabilities. To start using it, follow these steps:

1. Click Start ➤ Programs ➤ Perseus Applications ➤ Perseus SurveySolutions for the Web. Then click OK.

2. You will see the application window, including a floating, tabbed tool palette that gives you fast access to different parts of the program.

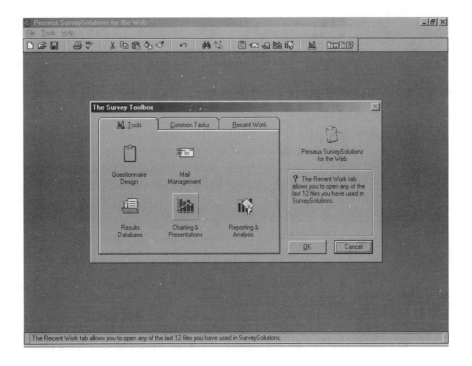

3. To learn how to use the program, select Perseus SurveySolutions Topics from the Help menu. A browser will open with the online documentation.

You will learn how to develop surveys that you can either post on a Web site or send via e-mail and then receive and compile the results automatically.

Learn about Surveys

What the programs assume is that you understand something about the nature of surveys. There are many subtleties that can affect the validity and usefulness of your results.

Though beyond the scope of this book, Perseus offers a tutorial on the basics of surveys at www.perseus.com/surveytips/Survey_101.htm.

58 Support a Virtual Office with Collaboration on Your Network

Working out of your home doesn't mean you are a professional misanthrope. Wherever the setting, business often means collaboration with others. Your network offers many mechanisms for working with others:

◆ Use a common whiteboard.

◆ Share applications.

◆ Manage common schedules and task lists.

All you need to do is use the proper software and have your Internet connection running.

Collaborate at a Distance with NetMeeting

Your network and NetMeeting provide a marvelous way of not only communicating with others but of reviewing ideas and even sharing applications. Here's how to do it:

1. Start NetMeeting.

2. Establish a call with your collaborator.

3. To use a common whiteboard, choose Whiteboard from the Tools menu, or click the Whiteboard icon on the Current Call Taskbar.

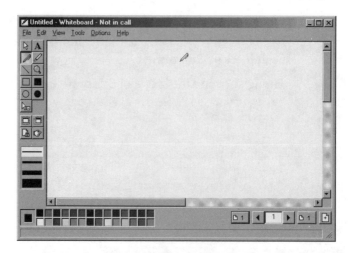

Follow these steps to share applications during a NetMeeting call:

1. Start the application.

2. Click the Current Call icon in the left frame of the NetMeeting window.

3. Click the Share icon at the top of the window, and then choose the application.

4. You can now demonstrate what is going on in the application.

5. To let someone else use your application, both you and the other person must click the Collaborate icon at the top of the screen.

Now you and the other person can take turns actually controlling the application.

Creating an Online Office with Yahoo!

Take the idea of a virtual office to its extreme and have a place that only exists online for meeting and conducting business. Some portal services, such as Yahoo!, let you create virtual offices, where you can

◆ Post messages to others in your company.

◆ Share a calendar with coworkers.

◆ Meet online.

◆ Use messaging to communicate with others.

With your network connection to the Internet, you get multiperson scheduling and online communications. This supplements your own network, which will provide the file and printer sharing you don't get online. To create your online office, follow these steps:

1. Start a browser.

2. Go to clubs.yahoo.com/office.

NOTE To use a virtual office, you and the people you work with have to create accounts with Yahoo! It doesn't cost anything, and you will be prompted to do so when you go to Yahoo's office site.

3. Log onto Yahoo!

4. Click the Create an Office button.

5. Click the Create My Connected Office button.

6. Provide the name of your company and the other information requested, and then click the Yes I Accept button.

Now you can add personnel as company members, check messages, and add events to the company calendar.

Keep Your Network and Home Secure

A look at one day's newspaper could convince anyone that security and safety are important: hackers breaking into networks, children being injured at home while parents are in other rooms, burglars robbing homes, baby-sitters mistreating their charges.

Legal action is useless in a way, because the damage is already done. But your network can actually help you protect yourself, your family and friends, and your belongings. Imagine doing the following:

- ◆ Protect your network when attached to the Internet.
- ◆ Keep an eye on the kids, even when they are in another room.
- ◆ Alert the authorities if someone tries to break into your home.
- ◆ Keep a record of how baby-sitters act.
- ◆ Prevent anyone from tampering with your personal files.

By using special hardware like sensors and cameras—or sometimes just software— you can achieve all this without having any experience. All you need is some patience.

59 Protect Your Files and Communications

Much of the data on your network or in your e-mails probably doesn't need extensive protection from prying eyes. If you are like most people, the lids on those eyes would quickly start drooping from boredom. But there are files and e-mails that you would not want visible to people, which is why it's always a good idea to have software to ensure your privacy.

There are two types you need. One is for e-mail and file attachments, whereas the other protects the privacy of files on your network.

Protect Communications with PGP Freeware

PGP, which stands for *pretty good protection,* is a commercial software package from Network Associates, but there is a free personal version, called PGP Freeware, available for downloading. It uses *encryption*, which is a technique that scrambles the contents of a file or message. Only someone who possesses the proper *key*—a special string of characters— can decode the message. To use PGP Freeware, you need to use either Eudora, Microsoft Outlook, Microsoft Outlook Express, or Microsoft Exchange for e-mail.

To install PGP Freeware, do the following:

1. First download the software from `web.mit.edu/network/pgp.html`. Save it into an empty directory.

WARNING There are legal restrictions on exporting this type of encryption technology out of the country, which is why encryption software is not included in this book's CD.

2. The file you receive is probably an archived file. You will need a program such as WinZip from Nicomac Computing or PKZip for Windows from PKWare to unarchive the file.

3. Highlight `Setup.exe` in Windows Explorer, and double-click it.

4. Follow the installation instructions you see on the screen.

5. At one point, you need to indicate what components you want to install. Leave everything checked except the e-mail program you do not use.

6. At another point, you have to indicate which network adapter you want to use with PGP. If you are using a proxy server, then highlight your outbound NIC. Only highlight the Dial-Up Networking adapter if you dial out directly from a PC.

After rebooting your computer, you will be able to use PGP Freeware. As soon as you have installed PGP, the program asks you whether you want to create a *key pair*. The *public* key only encrypts messages. You let others use it to send private messages to you. With the *private* key, you decrypt the messages so you can read them.

You can create a key pair at any time:

1. Click Start ➤ Programs ➤ PGP ➤ PGPkeys.

2. Click Next. Enter your name and e-mail address, and click Next twice.

3. For most uses, you can accept the key size value default. Click Next.

4. For added security, you can set the key pair to expire on a certain date. After that date, you will no longer be able to encrypt messages and will need to create a new key.

5. Fill in a password so you have access to your private key. Enter it a second time in the lower window, and click Next.

6. Now you have to either type or move your mouse around until the progress bar fills up. The typing or movement creates random information that the program needs. When the bar fills, click Next.

7. Wait until PGP indicates that it has generated your key pair. Click Next.

8. To be useful, PGP needs to file your public key to the main PGP server. If it isn't running, start your connection to the Internet.

9. Once connected to the Internet, be sure to check Send My Key to the Root Server Now, and then click Next.

10. When the software informs you that it has sent the key, click Next and then Finish.

You are now ready to use private e-mail. Another person gets a copy of your public key—either from a *certificate server* that stores such information or from you in a file or e-mail. That person encrypts a message with your key. No one else can now read that message. You control the process of encryption and decryption on your end with a toolbar that lets you perform the basic actions of PGP, including adding a digital signature that proves you are the person who sent the message.

Protect Chat Sessions

Many people use chat rooms regularly for social and even business reasons. If you want to protect the contents of your chat sessions from others, then you should try BetweenUs2 from TamoSoft, Inc. You and another person can have private Internet chats without having to manually encrypt and decrypt text. To install the program, follow these steps:

1. Go to www.tamos.com and follow the instructions for downloading BetweenUs2.

2. Save the file btweenus.zip to an empty directory. You will need a program such as WinZip from Nicomac Computing or PKZip for Windows from PKWare to unarchive the file.

3. Double-click setup.exe.

4. Click Yes to agree to the license, and then click Next.

5. Select Yes to ensure that you can completely uninstall the product if you decide to later. Click Next three times and then click Finish.

The program will automatically launch. You need to choose a nickname and to decide what type of encryption to use. Public key is a good choice, because someone intercepting the public key cannot decrypt any of the conversation. BetweenUs2 can also work with PGP.

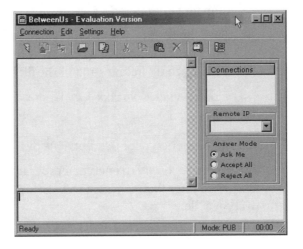

To make a connection, you can go to a public directory and register, so you and the other person can find each other.

1. Select Directory Service from the Connection menu.

2. Select the Current Directory tab, and click Connect to Directory.

3. Select the person you want to speak with.

Another approach is to provide the other party's IP address.

1. Each party selects Show IP Address from the Connection menu to see their own IP address.

2. Each sends to the other their IP address via e-mail.

3. Enter the other party's IP address in the Remote IP window, and click the connection icon.

You can then start chatting securely.

Protect Network Files

Although network operating systems offer some control over who can access files, a more thorough way of securing a file's content is to encrypt it.

Cryptext is a free software program that adds encryption to your operating system. It adds an encryption choice to the pop-up menu when you right-click a file. To use it, follow these steps:

1. Set your browser to www.pcug.org.au/~njpayne/, and choose a version for your operating system.

2. Save the file to an empty directory. You will need a program such as WinZip from Nicomac Computing or PKZip for Windows from PKWare to unarchive (unzip) the file.

3. Double-click cryptxxx.ext, where xxx is the current version number.

4. Click Yes.

You can now encrypt or decrypt a file by right-clicking it.

The first time you try to encrypt a program, you are prompted to enter a password. After that, Cryptext will ask for the password to encrypt or decrypt a file.

WARNING Do not forget your password. When encrypting a file, Cryptext eradicates the unencrypted version, so should you forget your password, you will be unable to read any of the encrypted files.

60 Protect Your Network from Power Problems

Anyone who has experienced it knows that losing power in the middle of doing something on a PC is highly annoying. That annoyance can extend into mind-numbing aggravation when your entire network grinds to a halt, especially if you are using it for important things such as

◆ Running your phone-answering system

◆ Monitoring household security

◆ Gaining access to your office

Keeping power available to your network can be important, indeed. You can take several steps to ensure your network stays running, depending on what causes an outage.

Guard Against Loose Cords and Fumbling Feet

You can shut down a computer by tripping over a power cord and pulling it from an outlet. Though some may find the point inane, it becomes far less silly the first time your network loses power because you are not the reincarnation of Fred Astaire.

The easy fix is to route power cables out of the way of the non-nimble. Put cords behind desks and other furniture. Desks designed for computers will have openings in the rear to run cables.

When cords tangle together, you also increase the chance that moving one will accidentally pull out another. Try to keep all your cables neat and tidy by using cable ties to bundle them together.

Use Surge Suppressers

Because computers and networks involve multiple power outlets, you may consider using extension cords to provide more power. Don't succumb to temptation, as extension cords become something else to trip over.

Better you should use power strips, as professionals do. These devices typically have one cord running to a wall outlet and have space for five or six plugs.

Purchase the type that has *surge suppression*. There are extraordinary circumstances, such as during a lightning strike, that a surge of electricity travels along power lines. At those times, equipment operating and connected to the wall outlet can be damaged or even outright destroyed. A surge suppresser will shut down the circuit in the face of a power spike. You may lose data when the PC goes off, but better that than losing the data *and* the computer.

When plugging a combination surge suppresser and power strip into the wall, be sure the power circuit in your home can handle the load. The total amount of power a circuit can deliver is the product of the *amps* for which it's rated and the voltage of the house current, typically 120V. You can determine the power consumption of an electrical device in a similar manner: multiply the household voltage by the current consumed.

NOTE For computer equipment, check the back of each device. There should be a plate that describes the number of amps the unit draws.

In the case of a typical 15-amp household circuit, the power capacity would be:

15 amps x 120 volts = 1,800 watts

That sounds like a lot until you realize that a circuit may run through several rooms and must power *everything* connected to it. Power consumption adds up quickly, as shown in Table 60.1:

TABLE 60.1 Power Consumption

Device	Power Consumption
PC Server	250 watts
Monitor	180 watts
Printer	120 watts
Scanner	100 watts

TABLE 60.1 Power Consumption (Continued)

Device	Power Consumption
Air Conditioner	500 watts
Six Lights at 100 watts	600 watts
Total Power	1750 watts

Without planning ahead, you could find yourself pushing the power limits of a circuit in your home. Short of upgrading your home's circuitry, the best offense is a good defense. With a network, you can spread out the devices you use. For instance, connect the printer to another computer, and keep the scanner where it is. Another possibility is to be aware of what you use at the same time. For example, don't print and scan simultaneously, because that is when both consume the maximum amount of power.

Because telephone lines can direct lightning to your computer through an internal or external modem, look for surge suppressers that also offer telephone-line protection.

Keep Things Running with a UPS

You could glue cords in place and carefully plan how many electrical devices you can run at one time, but you are out of luck if the source of power goes out. A particularly virulent storm or excess demand during the summer can result in brown-outs or even a complete loss of electricity.

A type of device that is worth its weight in gold is an *uninterruptable power supply,* or UPS. Think of the device as a high-capacity battery with an intelligent switch. So long as an outlet provides power, the UPS passes the power to the PC while also charging its own battery.

On losing power into the home, the UPS senses the problem and flips its internal switch, powering the PC on the fully charged battery.

As with surge suppressers and electrical circuits in the home, a UPS has only so much capacity. The closer your devices get to the rated capacity, the less time you are likely to have in case of power loss. Here's how to pick one:

1. Read the vendor's power rating for the UPS and the amount of time it can run off the battery.

2. List the equipment that you need to keep running. At the least, this would include a PC and a monitor.

3. Determine the power consumption of each.

4. Add the power consumptions together, and see how they compare to the UPS rating.

5. If the sum of the power consumptions is greater than the UPS rating, find a larger UPS.

A UPS won't solve all your potential power headaches. It can only run a short period of time, which is limited when power is out for an extended length of time. But that should be enough time to go around and let systems shut down gracefully, saving your data.

Many UPSs have a feature that will shut down a computer automatically and save whatever work was going on at the time. This is important because you won't be around the home all the time while your computer is on.

61 Put a Firewall between Your Network and the Internet

Hackers may have turned the bulk of their attention to large corporations, but that is no guarantee that someone won't decide to target home networks. There have even been destructive programs that crawled around the Internet, moving from one machine to others it could find.

The solution is to put a firewall up between your network and the Internet. This becomes more important as cable and DSL connectivity can leave your network connected to the Internet 24 hours a day.

How Firewalls Work

Firewalls aren't impenetrable barricades so much as a fancy electronic sleight-of-hand. They keep your home network separate from the Internet, yet they let the two communicate when necessary.

If an attempt at communication does not meet with the guidelines you set, the firewall rejects the information. Firewalls can use several strategies, including the following:

Proxy servers   Acting as a go-between, the firewall moves messages back and forth between the Internet and your network without letting the Internet see your real network addresses.

Packet filters   The firewall examines each packet of data and decides what may pass and what may not.

Circuit level gateways   The firewall receives messages for users, verifies the origin of the messages, and then decides whether it can safely pass them to the people on your network. If so, it forwards them to the appropriate users. There is never a real physical circuit between your network and someone on the Internet.

Application gateways   Application gateways are like circuit-level gateways, but they also combine features of a packet filter and actually examine the data as it comes through.

There are both hardware and software firewalls. The hardware firewalls can be difficult to configure, but the software firewalls are only as secure as the operating system on which they run.

Add a Firewall to Your Network

Practically speaking, a firewall is meant as a deterrent. If someone is highly skilled and bound and determined to cause you misery, they will. You could spend far too much time and money trying to protect yourself. Choose, instead, to chart a course of reasonable security, and remember that there is just too little prestige for a hacker to break into your network.

If you are running proxy server software, then you already have some degree of firewall protection. By the nature of the application, the proxy server keeps your network's real addresses secret from the Internet at large.

 You can also add some protection over and above the proxy server. SyShield from Sybergen Networks, for example, is a shareware product that

◆ Analyzes data packets

◆ Closes Internet connections if it detects hacking attempts

◆ Logs Internet access

◆ Lets users set security policies

You can choose the level of security you want, and the application works with proxy sharing.

To install the program, use this procedure:

1. Install the program with the user interface on the CD accompanying this book, or install manually by double-clicking the file SyShield.exe in the directory \Keep Network Secure\SyShield\ on the CD.

2. Click Yes, then Next twice, and finally, click Finish.

3. After installing itself, the software tests the connection you are using, so be sure you are connected to the Internet.

4. When the testing is done, click OK to restart your system.

5. To start SyShield, click Start ➤ Program ➤ SyShield ➤ SyShield.

The software now starts watching traffic from the Internet.

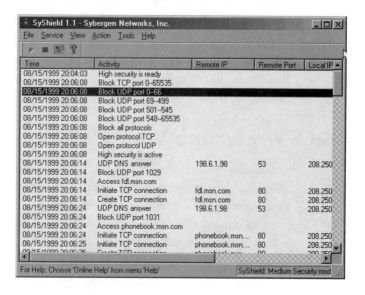

You can set security level from ultra-high, which results in blocking everything from the Internet to disabling security totally. The former might sound odd, as disconnecting from your ISP would have the same result, but there may be times, such as when you are backing up or when your children are home but you are not, that you will want to restrict Internet traffic. Follow these steps to set a regular time for high security:

1. Start SyShield.

2. Select Settings from the Tool menu.

3. Click the Security Schedule tab.

4. Set the beginning and ending times for automatic high security, or disable this feature by clicking the box.

You now have an added level of security above that offered by a proxy server.

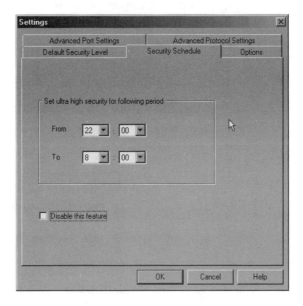

62 Get Control of Your Passwords

If you use the Internet often, you will undoubtedly find yourself needing to create passwords to get onto certain sites. Using the same password is a poor idea, but coming up with passwords and then remembering them can be a chore.

With the following programs, you can eliminate those problems.

Generate Random Passwords

A secret to keeping passwords secure is to use ones that are jumbles of characters that have no meaning. You could create your own passwords, but why not let a program do it for you?

Password Generator is a program that creates passwords for you. You provide a number between 4 and 24 to designate the length of password you want. The program creates a password by picking a mix of numbers and letters.

To use Password Generator, follow these steps:

1. Copy the file `passgen.exe` from the \Keep Network Secure\Password Generator\ directory on the CD included with this book to your network file server.

2. You can run the program from any client on your network. Just use Windows Explorer to find the program, and double-click it.

3. Type a number from 4 to 24 in the top box.

4. Press the button, and read the password from the bottom box.

You can use the password with any Web site or program, so long as you keep track of what it is.

Track Your Passwords

Even if you don't use complex passwords, remembering when to use each can be confusing. There are products, though, that can manage the password dilemma for you.

Password Keeper for Windows 95/NT lets you

◆ Use a single password for access to all your passwords.

◆ Store URLs for Web sites for fast access.

◆ Copy passwords to the clipboard and then to other programs.

◆ Store passwords for multiple people.

All you have to do is remember your single password to the program, and the other passwords are taken care of for you. To install Password Keeper, use this procedure:

1. Install the program with the user interface on the CD accompanying this book, or install manually by double-clicking the file PassKeep_Setup.exe in the directory \Keep Network Secure\Password Keeper\ on the CD.

2. Follow the directions on the screen. Keep note of which file the program uses to install the software. Because it only installs files in one directory, you can use this program over your network.

3. The software will present a tabbed window with various options, such as creating a desktop icon. After you set things the way you want, click OK.

4. You need to create a Password Keeper document by clicking New under the File menu and then choosing where to store it.

NOTE Users on your network can keep their passwords in separate documents, which are all locked by single passwords.

5. To add a password, select Add Account from the Edit menu.

6. Fill in all the information. You can have the program create a password if you don't have one.

Now you can store different passwords for different URLs without having to remember a single one of them.

63 Turn a Network into a Home Security System with ActiveHome

Networks are good not only for computer security but for running a security system for your home. You can

- ◆ Put sensors on doors and windows.

- ◆ Monitor motion in a room.

- ◆ Remotely turn the security system on and off.

You can use products, such as those from X10, to integrate household security with a networked computer and actually automate the entire process.

ActiveHome is a home automation system that can manage security, lights, and even entertainment systems. It uses a combination of wireless and power line networking technology to connect your network to everything else in your home.

To install the program, you need an open serial port on your server. Follow these steps:

1. Install the program with the user interface on the CD accompanying this book, or install manually by double-clicking the file setup67.exe in the directory \Keep Network Secure\ActiveHome\ on the CD.

2. Double-click on Intro.exe.

3. Select Yes to create backups of replaced files in case you want to uninstall the software in the future, and then click Next twice.

4. ActiveHome defaults to using the COM 2 serial port. To see if it is available, click Start ➤ Settings ➤ Control Panel. Double-click System.

5. Select the Device Manager tab.

6. Click the plus sign next to Ports.

7. Look to see if COM 2 is listed. If it is, choose another available COM port number. The COM ports are numbered from 1 to *N*, where *N* is the number of serial ports on the computer. ActiveHome restricts you to choosing from COM 1, COM 2, COM 3, and COM 4.

8. Select Yes to load the software when Windows starts, and then click Next.

Before you can use the product, you have to restart the PC. But to do anything with the software, you need some specific hardware. The CD accompanying this book provides details of how you can get an introductory hardware kit for under $6.

There are two types of special hardware you need—controllers, which accept directions from the PC and transmit them, and modules, which receive the directions and operate devices accordingly. For security control, these devices are sensors that detect whether doors or windows have been opened or whether there is movement in a room.

Follow X10's directions for installing the sensor hardware, which typically involves mounting the sensor and a connected wireless transmitter that broadcasts to a security monitor. You connect this, in turn, to a computer interface for the PC.

To connect the PC running ActiveHome to your security equipment, follow these steps:

1. Exit all programs, and turn off the PC.

2. Remove the PC's plug from the power outlet.

3. Put batteries in the ActiveHome controller that plugs into the wall outlet.

4. Connect the phone-jack end of the supplied serial cable into the bottom of the controller.

5. Connect the serial connector end of the cable to the serial port for the COM port you chose earlier.

6. Plug the controller into the wall outlet.

7. Plug the PC's power cord into the controller.

8. Restart the PC.

To use ActiveHome, Click Start ➢ Programs ➢ Home Control ➢ Active-Home. The first time you start the software, you may see images of how to install the software. Press the Escape button to clear the screen each time you see an image.

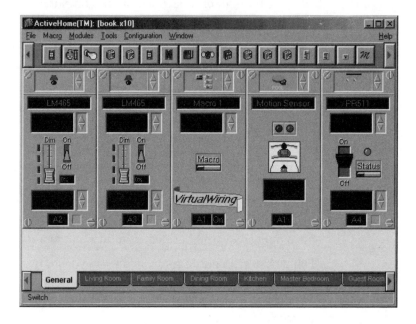

As you can see, you control monitors through illustrations of the devices. The biggest advantage of the ActiveHome software, other than remote monitoring of your security system, is running macros, which are little programs you use to control lights and applications. Although some of the security equipment only works through the security console, other equipment can report to the PC. So you could, for example, have a motion detector start a PC macro that will turn on a set of lights while another detector notifies the security monitor to telephone for help.

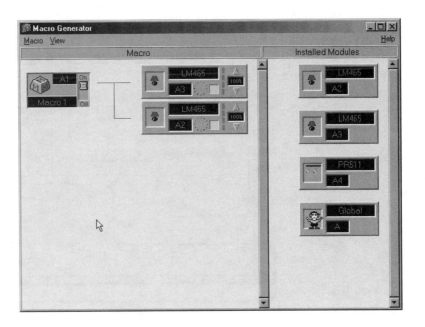

64 Control the Lights with ActiveHome When You Are Away

It's better to scare a burglar off than to call for help. When you aren't at home, you can have ActiveHome control your lights with the following steps:

1. Determine which lights you want to control.

2. Draw a diagram grouping the lights that will go on together.

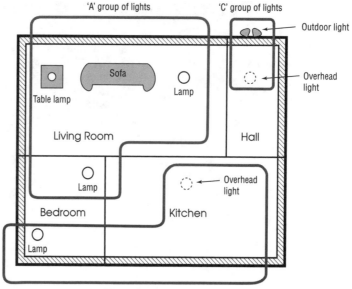

3. Use an X10-compatible lamp module for each lamp, wall-switch module, or screw-in lamp module for each overhead light.

4. Turn off the power at the circuit breaker or fuse for each overhead light, and install the wall switch that will control it.

5. Plug the lamps into the lamp modules, and then plug the lamp modules into wall outlets.

6. Each module can be set with a circuit letter and an identifying number. All lights that are supposed to turn on together should have the same circuit letter, though with different identifying numbers.

7. Create macros to trigger when lamps should light and at what intensity.

8. Double-click each macro under ActiveHome to configure time and date triggers for the lights.

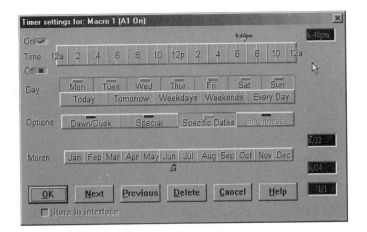

For example, you might want a table lamp and some track lights in one group and an overhead light and a fluorescent light in another. Each could go on and off on different time schedules, giving a random pattern that would look like someone was at home.

You can also decide to set each light to an individual schedule, too:

1. Select Timer Settings under the Modules menu.

2. Select a module, and click OK.

3. Set on and off times for the lights.

This way you have a maximum of control. You can also use this feature to turn lamps on automatically before you get home at night.

NOTE If you are away, configure lights to come on with a minute or two in between each, otherwise it will look as though everyone in the house takes part in a strange ritual of turning on separate lights in different parts of your home at precisely the same time.

65 See What Is Happening at a Distance with Video

There are good reasons someone might use video to see what is happening elsewhere.

◆ You can get a clear view of who is at a door without advertising that you are at home.

◆ If you are busy, a quick view at a computer monitor lets you know if you need to stop what you are doing.

◆ An injury that could make walking difficult might leave you wanting to see who was at a door without getting up.

◆ It lets you keep an eye on kids while doing something else.

◆ You can configure a camera to capture pictures of someone entering your home and be alerted remotely.

◆ With the right set-up, you can actually see what's happening in your home during the day.

You can prepare for any of these cases by setting up video in your home. There are at least three approaches you can use:

◆ Create an internal Web cam.

◆ Use videoconferencing after pointing the camera at whatever interests you.

◆ Work with wireless cameras that broadcast to your PC.

In addition, there are situations in which a video camera might be used in combination with something else.

Create Your Own Web Cam

With today's network technology, you have the bandwidth to deliver live video using the Internet technology called *Web cams*. These are typically video cameras connected to a Web server that can provide images all over the world. But you can also use Web cams in your home.

Anywhere you can situate a video camera and a computer, you can have live video:

◆ Mount a small video camera near your front door, run a cable into the house, and see who is ringing your doorbell.

◆ Put a camera by the pool, and have a view of what the kids are doing while you get some work done.

◆ Point a camera at the stove to see whether something starts to boil over so you can leave the kitchen when you can't stand the heat.

◆ Run a Web server on the Internet with a Web cam so you can see what is happening at home during the day.

◆ Save video to the hard drive to check on how the baby-sitter did with the kids.

You have plenty of network bandwidth to get good images in your home. A telephone-based network provides up to 10Mbps bandwidth. An Ethernet network can give you upwards of 100Mbps. To put this in perspective, that's about ten to 100 times more capacity than a cable or DSL Internet hook-up—more than enough to get decent images.

Here are the general steps to using a Web cam with a Windows 98 PC as the host:

1. Pick a networked computer close to the site you want to see.

2. Be sure the PC has a video capture or TV tuner board.

3. Load Microsoft Personal Web Server onto the machine. (See "40. Create Your Own Web Server.")

4. Install the Web cam software.

5. Include the appropriate code in an HTML page.

6. View the cam from another networked PC with a browser.

It sounds much more complicated than it is. On the CD accompanying this book, you will find an evaluation version of Webcam32, a shareware program that lets you display video output on a Web page. Its documentation provides the HTML code you need to add to a Web page to show the video.

To install Webcam32, do the following:

1. Install the program with the user interface on the CD accompanying this book, or install manually by double-clicking the file `webcam32.exe` in the directory `\Keep Network Secure\Webcam32\` on the CD.

2. Click Next, then Yes, and then Next again.

3. You have to restart the computer to let the software work. You can either choose to do it now or take care of it later.

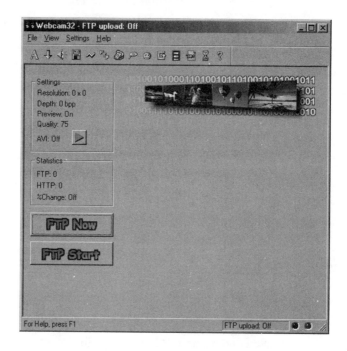

You now need to decide on a number of options:

◆ Either load single file shots via FTP (File Transfer Protocol) to the Web page or stream full video.

◆ Configure TCP/IP particulars.

◆ If you stream full video, pick the mechanism by which to do it.

For these, and other issues, see the full Webcam32 documentation at `www.surveycorp.com/webcam32`. To stream video, pay special attention to the Streaming Video section of the documentation, especially the sections on JavaCamPush, which is a special java program that can send video from Webcam32 to a browser.

Use Video Teleconferencing to See Video

If the thought of dealing with a Web server and video feeds makes your teeth ache, then video teleconferencing may provide an answer. Review "46. Put a Face behind the Words with Video Phoning." Not a word in the section suggests what the video camera on the far end of a connection specifically has to be facing.

Here's how you would use video teleconferencing—with NetMeeting as an example—to provide the ability to see things elsewhere in your home:

1. Set up at least one computer with a video card and camera.

2. Run NetMeeting, and look at the video available.

3. Point the camera at the area you want to see later.

4. Set up a NetMeeting connection between this computer and another computer in your home.

5. If you want the video to be unnoticeable, turn off the monitor of the PC you use as the video host.

You can now go to the other PC and look through the NetMeeting connection you established. The disadvantages are that to see the video from another location on your network, you would have to end the call and start another call from the next PC, which means accepting the incoming call from the video server. There is a way around this, though:

1. Select Options from the Tools menu on the copy of NetMeeting running on the video server.

2. Select the General tab.

3. Select Automatically Accept Incoming Calls.

4. Click OK.

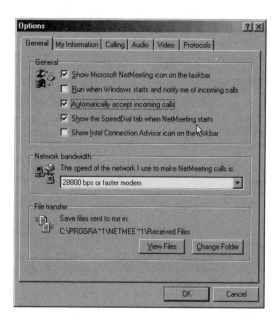

This way, you can start calls from any other location on your network.

Transmit Video in Your Home

Another relatively easy approach to seeing video is to send it from one location to another via high-frequency radio transmission. There are a number of products that provide this capability.

One is MicroSentinel from Security Data Networks, Inc. Unlike Web cam and video teleconferencing, you don't need a video capture board on a PC to see video. MicroSentinel comes with a camera and microphone unit that transmits a signal at 2.4GHz to a receiver that passes the image and sound through a cable to the PC's parallel port.

Using a system like this, you cannot easily move the image over your network. But because you have multiple PCs, you do have your choice of where to set up the receiver. It's also not difficult to move.

WARNING The frequency that MicroSentinel uses is similar to that used by many wireless networking products, which could cause interference.

MicroSentinel also has some security features that you will find convenient:

♦ The camera has a motion detector that can instruct the MicroSentinel PC software to record when something moves in the room.

♦ You can record only at particular times.

♦ The software can upload images to an FTP server, which means it can act as a Web cam either for the Internet or your own network.

♦ It can notify you by e-mail or pager when it detects motion.

♦ You can use up to four different cameras and have the receiver automatically switch from one to the other.

To install the system, follow these steps:

1. Connect a power supply to the camera. Press the top button on the back of the unit until the light under the number 1 is lit.

2. Connect a power supply to the receiver, and then use the parallel cable to connect the receiver to the PC's printer port.

3. Turn the receiver on, and press the number 1 button on the side.

4. Put the software CD in the CD drive. If it doesn't start automatically, then click Start ➤ Run, and type **D:Setup.exe**, where D is the drive letter for your CD-ROM. Then click OK.

5. Click Next four times, and then click Finish.

Once installed, you can see the video on your screen any time you click Start ➤ Programs ➤ MicroSentinel ➤ MicroSentinel. By clicking the Options button, you can set options to e-mail images, upload images to a Web site, and record video when the camera detects motion, among other things.

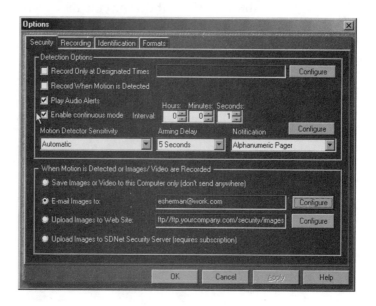

Make Your Network a Home Productivity Tool

Exotic applications are all well and good, but it's the everyday use that makes a network truly valuable:

◆ Get an update of the weather in your area or other places.

◆ Stop searching for the phone-number list of a child's classmates by having them, along with information for all other contacts, on your network.

◆ Forget about having paper and pencil around with a network phone-message system.

◆ Put your recipes and meal plans on a network server.

◆ Automate temperature controls and appliances.

Your network can perform tasks from keeping household schedules and chore lists to having phone numbers and messages at your fingertips. It can even turn on the lights and coffeepot when you wake.

66 Keep a Central Network Phone List for Everyone

Forget slips of paper, contact sheets from school, and the 15-year-old address book you have carried for years. If having phone numbers on a computer is convenient, keeping them in a network phone book is revolutionary:

◆ Everyone at home can find phone numbers when they need them.

◆ There's never a question as to what piece of paper houses the address for someone.

◆ There's no fighting over notebooks and sheets of paper, because everyone can get access to phone numbers at the same time.

Although there are many phone-book applications on the market, most of them are intended for a single computer. When you are using the program, someone else can't get access to the data.

The solution is to use a networked application. Besides telephone answering and faxing capabilities, Call Center also manages shared phone books. To get the feature, though, you must register the software.

Though Call Center has a bias toward business users, the product will work fine for home use. After installing the product according to the directions in "47. Put an Answering Service on Your Network with Call Center," do the following:

1. Click Start ➢ Programs ➢ COMponents ➢ Call Center to start the program.

2. Click the top icon on the left side of the Call Center screen. You will see the PhoneList screen.

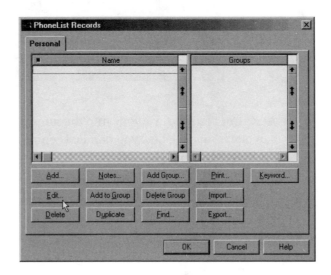

3. You can now start adding names to your phone list. Select the Personal tab to enter basic data, such as an address and phone number. Under some of the other tabs, you can enter other information, such as a pager number and an e-mail address.

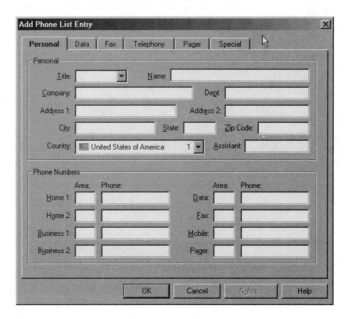

Aside from putting everyone into the same phone book, there are ways you can better manage how you handle keeping track of people. One is the business concept of keeping notes about your conversations with people. To do this, follow these steps:

1. Highlight someone's name.

2. Click on the Notes button.

3. Type in the note and a title for it.

4. Click Close.

Though typically a business function, notes help you track conversations with others. Another handy feature is the ability to put people into groups. Say, for example, that you are on a committee for a civic organization. You can place people on the committee under specific catagories:

1. Click Add Group.

2. Type in the group name.

3. Click OK.

4. Highlight each of the people who should be in the group, and click Add to Group. Select the group for the list that pops up, and click OK.

5. In the PhoneList Records screen, you can right-click a group name, and select Expand to see all the people in that group.

You can also create multiple phone books. This lets you keep a common phone list for everyone as well as personal phone lists. To create a new phone book, use this procedure:

1. Click Start ➤ Programs ➤ COMponents ➤ COMponent WorkSpace.

2. Select Create/Edit Phonebooks under the File menu.

3. Click New.

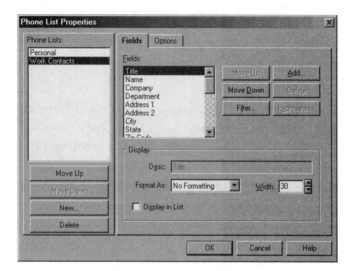

4. Choose whether you want a phone list that will reside just on one computer or a shared list available to all.

5. Select the directory in which to store the phone book. For shared lists, this will typically be in the Program Files\V3COM\PHONE directory on the server. Click OK.

6. Create a name for the phone book, and click OK.

7. You can choose what fields of information to display for the records. For example, for a list of work contacts, you might decide to show the name of each person's assistant.

8. Select formatting—such as telephone or initial capital letter—if appropriate.

9. Click OK, and then exit COMponent WorkSpace.

Now when you click on the Display Phonebooks icon on the Call Center screen, you will see an additional tab for the new phone book.

67 Get All Your Phone Calls with a Network Phone Message System

How many times do you learn too late that a message about an important phone call found its way onto a piece of paper you never saw? With a home network, you can eliminate the problem. Every PC can become a phone answering station, without the need for paper or pencil. You can even solve the message problem in a number of different ways:

◆ E-mail the message.

◆ Use your network home intercom system.

◆ Enter phone messages in Ziata!

◆ Take Messages with Pink Notes Plus.

E-mail the Message

With a permanent Internet connection, such as cable or DSL, you can send an e-mail containing the phone message to someone else in your home. It may seem like swatting a fly with a barn, but it works.

If your household is using one e-mail account for everyone, you can still use the e-mail route. Use an e-mail proxy product, such as Wizmail from Lovdahl Consulting, to share the e-mail account. (See "39. Run Your Own E-mail System.") Because e-mail systems let you include both the actual e-mail address and the recipient's name, the e-mail proxy delivers the message to the right person.

Use Your Network Home Intercom System

There are times you take a phone message because someone is busy. If that person is using a networked computer, simply use the intercom functions the network makes available. (See "49. Create a Home Intercom System.") That way you can get messages to people right away and let them decide whether to take the call or not—while conveniently discharging your obligation. For example, everyone could run winpopup.exe to both send and receive messages on the monitor.

Enter Phone Messages in Ziata!

Even if you don't run a business out of your home, business-oriented software may still have a place in your home. Ziata! gives control over many aspects of business operations, including phone messaging. (To install, see "55. Network Your Vital Business Information with Ziata!")

When in the main screen of Ziata!, press Ctrl+E or double-click Take Phone Messages under the Telephone category. Ziata! uses e-mail to deliver messages as well as keeping a log of phone messages.

See "55. Network Your Vital Business Information with Ziata!" for more information on how to use the product.

Take Messages with Pink Notes Plus

Pink Notes Plus is a software application that lets you take phone messages and send them to other people on your network. The messages either pop up on someone's screen or go to a file for later reading.

Here's how to get Pink Notes Plus running on Windows 98 PCs on your network:

1. To install Pink Notes, copy the Pink Notes folder from \Network as Productivity Tool\Pink Notes on the CD to the hard drive of a networked PC. From there, double-click pnp102d3.exe.

2. Click Next five times, and then click Finish when the product is installed.

3. Check to see whether you have TCP/IP installed on each of the PCs. If not, install it. (See "19. Let Computers Talk with a Network Protocol.")

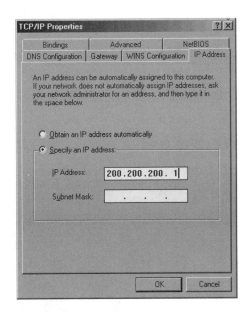

You are now ready to start Pink Notes Plus:

1. Click Start ➢ Programs ➢ Pink Notes Plus ➢ Pink Notes Plus.

2. Click Yes to accept the license.

3. Click OK.

4. Click the Address tab. Look at the IP Address section. If you see numbers there, go to step 12.

5. If you don't see an IP address, you will have to create one. The address consists of four numbers, each of which can take a value from 0 to 255. If you want, use a pattern of 200.200.200.X, where X is different for each PC on your network.

6. Click Start ➢ Settings ➢ Control Panel ➢ Network.

7. Highlight the protocol TCP/IP -> <NIC>, where <NIC> is the model NIC that the PC uses. Click Properties.

8. Select the IP Address tab.

9. Select Specify an IP address. Enter the IP address you created in Step 5.

WARNING The last part of an IP address should never be 0 or 255.

10. Ignore the Subnet Mask section.

11. Click OK twice.

12. Enter your first name.

13. Select the Display tab. Decide how you want to receive messages.

14. Click OK.

Your system tray now has an icon for Pink Notes Plus. To send a note, double-click that icon. Using the program is self-explanatory.

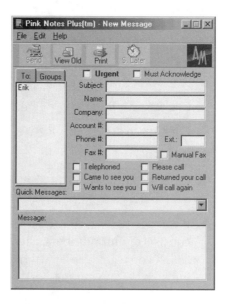

Use Windows CE Devices as Message Taking Stations

You may have phones in places where a PC isn't available, but that doesn't mean you should either give up on keeping network records or resign yourself to buying additional PCs.

Instead of keeping a full PC at each phone, try using hand-held Windows CE devices. They are compatible with some Ethernet NICs, so you can add the devices to your network if it runs on cable. Use the built-in version of Word to edit files, and you have a mini-note station. You can also use Windows CE to send e-mail.

NOTE You can find keyboards that work with Windows CE computers. The company Genovations, Inc. makes some that are small yet still offer a comfortable keyboard. The Compaq Aero 8000 is another solution—a CE computer with a full keyboard and large, bright screen, although it is more expensive.

68 Let Everyone Use the Same Shopping and To-Do Lists

Having common to-do and shopping lists makes great sense and certainly beats having the blind lead the uninformed:

◆ Household chores are in a place that everyone can see.

◆ Everyone can add to a shopping or grocery list easily.

◆ You can see what someone else is scheduled to do.

Using central lists is also one of the easiest things you can do on your network. It requires no extra software, just some agreements on how you add and check off items; for example, everyone might use one line per item and then delete the line when done.

Here's how to make your central lists work:

1. Select a location on your server's hard drive.

2. Create one directory to hold a to-do list and another for each shopping list.

3. One person—it doesn't matter who—opens either Notebook or WordPad, starts the list, and saves it to the network location.

Now everyone else can share the files. Be sure that each person saves the files so others can open them. Saving a file as a Word for Windows document can make it unavailable to someone using Notebook.

NOTE Because this is not a true multiuser solution, only one person can have a file open at a time. In a household setting, though, this should not prove a problem. It's unlikely there will be a run on learning who takes out the garbage.

69 Track Household Finances on Your Network

Whether you have your own family or live with roommates, there are always household expenses. Tracking them on your network makes much more sense than keeping records on a single computer or paper. You can make entries when you need to from where you are.

Having your own household financial center is easy:

1. Create a finance directory on your file server.

2. Install your household finance software on each PC where you might use it.

3. When given the option of picking the directory to install, choose your network finance directory.

Now you will be able to enter bills and payments wherever there is a networked computer.

Track Bills with Ncome and Xpense

 If you are happy writing your own checks and want a package that will tell you when you need to write them, then try installing Ncome and Xpense, a version of which can be found on the CD accompanying this book:

1. To install Ncome and Xpense, go to the directory \Network as Productivity Tool\Ncome and Xpense and copy the Ncome and Xpense folder to the hard drive of a networked PC. From there, launch the Setup.exe file.

2. Click Next and Yes.

3. You need to fill in the name and company fields and then click Next.

4. Click Browse, choose your finance directory, and then click Next twice.

5. Click Finish.

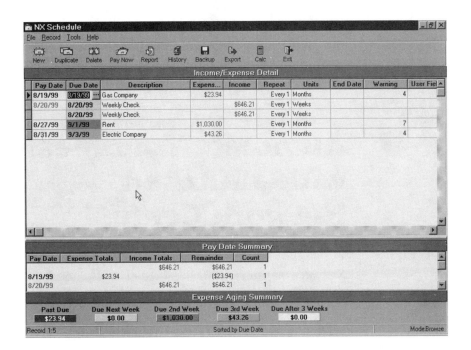

You can now start the program by clicking Start ➢ Programs ➢ Ncome and Xpense. When you first start the program, choose to see the introduction.

Entering data is like filling out a table, with amounts going into either expense or income as appropriate. To pay a bill, highlight it, and click the Pay Now icon.

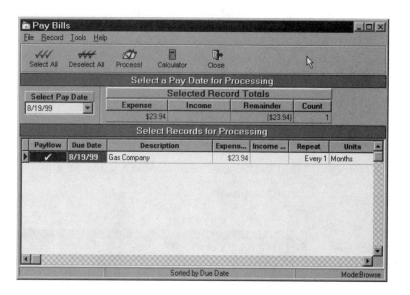

70

Automate Your Meals with a Kitchen Network Center

Networks may not take the heat out of the kitchen, but they can certainly keep you out of hot water when it comes to organizing. There are many things you can put onto your network that can help a culinary existence happen smoothly:

◆ Keep recipes on a recipe server.

◆ Manage your grocery lists.

◆ Create meal plans for the week.

◆ Check nutritional information on the food you cook.

With the to-do list approach described in "68. Let Everyone Use the Same Shopping and To-Do Lists" and recipe and culinary software, you should be all set.

Before starting anything, though, you need a computer in the kitchen. Then you can start adding software.

Track Recipes and Build Shopping Lists with Now You're Cooking!

If you are going to cook and have a network, you might as well *really* use a computer in the kitchen. Now You're Cooking! is an application that combines

- ◆ Recipe management
- ◆ Nutritional information
- ◆ Recipe downloading from the Web
- ◆ Menu and shopping-list creation

An evaluation of the software is on the CD that accompanies this book. Follow these steps to install Now You're Cooking!:

1. Using the interface on the CD accompanying this book, install Now You're Cooking! To install manually, go to the directory\Network as Productivity Tool\Now You're Cooking!\ on the CD and double-click Setup.exe.

2. Click Next and then Accept.

3. Click the Browse button, and choose a directory on your file server. Then click Next.

4. Select Yes to keep back-up copies of files, and then click Next twice.

5. Click Finish.

You are now ready to start the program by clicking Start ➤ Programs ➤ Now You're Cooking (32-bit) ➤ Now You're Cooking (32-bit).

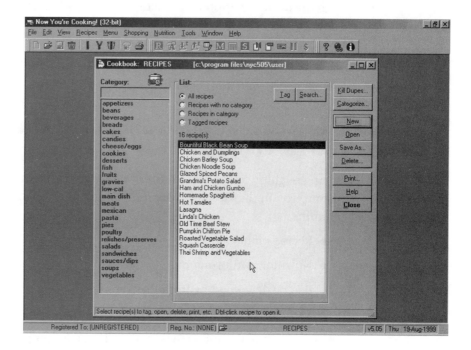

The first time you start the program, click OK to give it permission to create a nutrition database. Some of the things you can do are

◆ Create specific cookbooks.

◆ Import recipes from other cookbook programs.

◆ Categorize recipes.

◆ Show nutritional information.

Now You're Cooking! is easy to use, and the best way to get acquainted is to poke about and try different things with the recipes that come with the software. For example, by selecting Analysis from the Nutrition menu, you can get a nutritional analysis of whatever recipe is currently displayed.

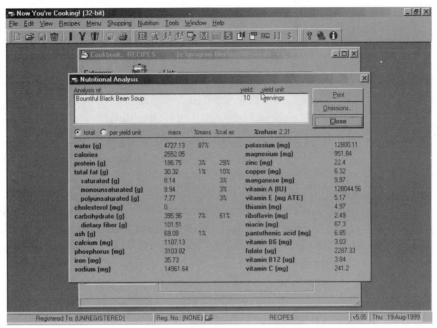

71 Automate Your Home with X10 and Your Network

Your network can not only handle messages and files but let you manage all manners of things in your home, such as

- ◆ Lights
- ◆ Draperies
- ◆ Appliances
- ◆ Thermostats

Using products from X10 Ltd., as well as from companies making compatible devices, you can control virtually any type of electrical device. The basic steps are

1. Install Set ActiveHome software (on the CD accompanying this book) on your network server.

2. Connect a serial port of your PC to an X10-compliant controller plugged into an outlet. One source of them is www.x10.com.

3. Connect an electrical device in your home to an appropriate X10 module.

4. Configure the modules in ActiveHome.

ActiveHome running on the server will control your household for you. Should you want to take a more active hand during the day and aren't at the server, use Traveling Software's LapLink Professional to control the server from another computer on the network, and then use ActiveHome remotely.

Control Your Lights

As "64. Control the Lights with ActiveHome when You Are Away" explains, you can have lights go on and off at certain times and even turn lights on in the presence of motion. This is useful not only for household security but for convenience:

◆ Have lights in your home go on before you return from errands or work at night, so you don't have to stumble about in the dark.

◆ As unpleasant as it seems at the time, having bedroom lights automatically turn on when it's time to wake can do much to propel you from bed.

◆ Enable lights connected to motion detectors at certain hours, so if you find yourself trotting over to the kitchen for a late night snack, you can have light greeting you.

◆ If you or the people who live with you constantly forget to turn off certain lights late at night, you can have a network server running ActiveHome turn them off for you.

◆ Put lights on a dimmer, adjusting their brightness at different times of the day.

Controlling your lights with your network and ActiveHome adds convenience and can even save you money.

Control Your Drapes

Perhaps you are busy on the computer and realize the sun is streaming through your home's windows and threatening to bake your pet parakeet. You could get up and walk to the drapes or have your computer take care of the problem for you.

There are other reasons you might want to automate your draperies:

◆ Make an empty dwelling look as though someone is home.

◆ Have the curtains open in the morning to help wake you up.

◆ Either let light in or shield a room from the sun's heat by having the drapes open and close at certain times of the day.

ActiveHome from X10 can control your drapes by taking the following steps:

1. Obtain a motorized drapery unit from a home-improvement store.

2. Use the X10 Universal Module UM506.

3. If the drapery control normally works with a single button push, configure the UM506 to act as a momentary contact closure. Otherwise, time how long it takes for the draperies to open or close, and set the operation of the UM506 in ActiveHome for that amount of time.

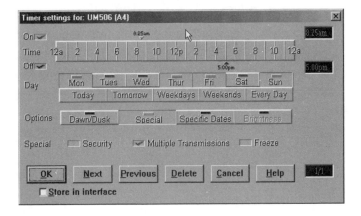

4. Plug the UM506 into a wall socket, and plug the drapery motor into the module.

You are now ready to have your curtains open and close at your bidding.

Control Your Appliances

There are plenty of reasons why you might like appliances to turn on and off on schedule:

◆ Have the coffee maker brew a pot in time for you to wake in the morning.

◆ When late-night television viewers doze off while watching TV, have your network turn the TV off.

◆ Set sprinkler systems to turn on early in the morning and finish before you leave.

To make all this and more happen, use the appropriate modules from X10 and other vendors with compatible products. For example, perhaps you have a coffeepot without a self-timer. You can have it start your coffee in the morning by following these steps:

1. The night before, prepare the coffee to brew.

2. Use the proper module. For a two-prong, polarized plug (one prong is larger than the other), use an AM486. For a three-prong, grounded plug, use an AM466.

3. Select the kitchen tab on ActiveHome.

4. Select Appliance Module from the Modules menu. Choose the proper module, an AM486 in this example.

5. Press any key to clear the image of the controller.

6. Click the black timing rectangle (next to the Up and Down arrows).

7. Set the on and off times and days for the coffeepot, and then click OK.

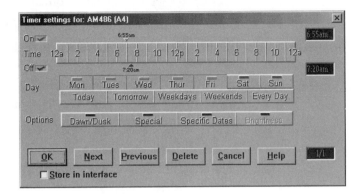

8. Turn the switch on the AM486 screen image to the On position.

In this example, your coffee starts to brew at 6:55, and the coffeepot turns itself off at 7:20.

Control Your Thermostat

It's easy to waste money by having heating and cooling systems on when no one needs them. For example, you leave your air conditioner off to conserve electricity when away from home and then have to wait an hour for it to cool your home when you finally return.

With an X10 thermostat set-back controller, you can solve both these problems. Instead of replacing an existing thermostat, the set-back controller supplies a small amount of heat under the thermostat. This makes the thermostat react as though the room was hotter than it actually is, resulting in the thermostat either turning off the heat or turning on the air-conditioning.

You can increase the apparent heat by as much as 15 degrees. By using the set-back controller with ActiveHome software, you can create macros to change the temperature at particular times of the day. For example, you might have the set-back controller leave the heat off until shortly before you come back from work:

1. Leave the thermostat at its usual setting.

2. Configure the set-back controller to warm the thermostat by 10 degrees. Because it seems hotter to the controller, the heat doesn't go on.

3. Have a macro keep the set-back controller on while you are gone.

4. The macro should turn the controller off, which will let the thermostat realize that the heat should go on, before you get back from work. Have the controller shut off long enough before your return so the heater can warm your home.

Now when you open the front door, you'll be greeted with warmth—and a lower fuel or power bill. With a slight change in approach, you can do something similar with air-conditioning:

1. If you have central air-conditioning controlled by a thermostat, set the thermostat higher than normal while you are away. This will make hotter temperatures seem like something desired.

2. Configure the set-back controller to warm the thermostat by 10 degrees.

3. Have a macro keep the set-back controller *off* when you are away.

4. Keeping in mind the time necessary to cool your home, have the macro turn the set-back controller *on* before you return.

By having the set-back controller go on, the thermostat reacts as though the room has suddenly become hotter and, in reaction, turns the air conditioning on. When you get home, simply turn the thermostat back down to the level you find comfortable.

If the air conditioner is a stand-alone unit without an external thermostat, use an appliance module. Instead of setting thermostats, a macro simply turns the air conditioner on before you get home.

Set Up a Learning Lab for Children of All Ages

Networks can be about much more than connecting to the Internet or running the coffeepot and telephone. There is much anyone can learn with a home network:

- ◆ Create educational areas on your server to improve basic skills.

- ◆ Develop an educational environment where your children can cooperate with their classmates and work on school projects.

- ◆ Improve your musical knowledge and even compose your own pieces.

- ◆ Study the stars with a virtual planetarium.

- ◆ Participate in the search for extraterrestrial intelligence.

- ◆ Get an advanced degree with distance education programs or develop knowledge in the profitable field of data networks.

In fact, there's so much a network can offer in education, you might nickname yours the school of hard pings.

72 Let Your Kids Do Homework over the Internet

Problems of unsuitable material for children aside, the Internet is a fine resource for doing homework. From finding research material quickly to locating photographs that students can add to their reports, there are immense resources online. You can find

- ◆ Searchable texts of famous literature

- ◆ Explanations of science topics

- ◆ People who can answer questions on different subjects

- ◆ Specialized research categories

All this is available 24 hours a day, with no need to go to a library or wait for someone to finish with a particular book. A high-bandwidth connection between your network and the Internet, such as DSL or cable, can greatly speed up the process. There are good sites for particular areas of interest as well as those covering education in the home. However, you do need to take some care.

Find Educational Sites

Although tremendous resources are available on the Internet, it can be useful to find sites that can provide extended information on a particular theme. Check major search engines, such as Yahoo.com, before you let your children loose. Go through each site and be sure that you consider it appropriate.

For example, Michael's craft stores have a site (`www.michaels.com/kids/kid-main.html`) that is not offensively commercial and that offers crafts projects, including full patterns available online, which can help develop artistic skills. The Cowdisley Education Group (`www.geocities.com/Paris/Opera/4929/`), is on the opposite end of the spectrum, with online painting lessons, including figure painting, that are more suited to adults. Yet both can be found in a search engine when looking for art education.

The lesson is to review the contents of pages before you pass them on to your children. Pay special attention to pages containing links, because the same care someone brings to creating a child-friendly Web site often does not extend to thoroughly examining linked pages.

You might also want to look at parent and teacher resources, which can indirectly help your children by making you smarter about education. One good site is Stufo.com (`www.stufo.com`), with resources for home schooling, parents, and teachers.

Take Care of Your Kids

Even after selecting sites, you still want to safeguard your children. Be sure to review some of the suggestions in "41. Protect Your Kids on the Internet."

The main rule is never to become complacent. As fast as you can work to shield kids from the vagaries of the world, they can as quickly find ways around restrictions just to see what all the fuss is about.

73 Have Children Do School Work over Your Network

It is amazing how quietly work can proceed among children when they aren't in the same room. With a network, you can set up an educational area, develop projects, and even let kids work together when it's too late for them to be out and about.

Set Up an Educational Server

Set aside space on your network server to become the educational center. You can house software that helps children and adults learn.

For children, consider creating a directory for each grade, with subdirectories for each student and then for particular subjects.

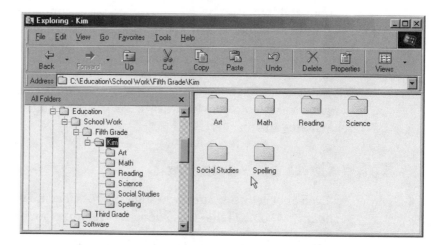

With this approach, you can keep an archive of the work children do separate from that of siblings who go through the same grade at different times.

Develop School Projects on the Network

Networks can be terrific tools in school projects. From letting kids experiment with programming to scanning maps for geography and creating electronic artwork, your networked computers can help children explore. Here's an example of what you can do:

1. Create a Project folder in the appropriate Subject folder in the right Grade folder.

2. In the Project folder, create a subfolder with the project title. Within the Project folder, have a Resources folder and a Work folder.

3. As children research their projects, they should save files and information in the Resources folder. Because Windows 95 and 98 support long filenames, use them: give each saved file a descriptive title.

4. Information found in books, magazines, and other print sources can go into a word-processor file.

5. Any writing and graphics work for a written or oral report then goes into the Work folder.

Because the files are logically named and are on a network server, you can add material you may come across that your kids would find useful or interesting.

Let Kids Work Together on the Network

Your kids can work with their schoolmates, no matter how late it is or where they live, when you let them dial into your network. The students can have common access to project files, work through problems together, or even just check in with each other.

Here are the steps to take to have kids work together:

1. Configure a Windows Dial-Up server as described in "22. Remotely Access Your Home Network with a Windows 98 Dial-Up Server."

2. Provide a password that unlocks only the appropriate education areas on your network. You want kids from the outside to work with yours, not play on your network.

3. Be sure everyone is using NetMeeting to have the chat and white board features for collaboration, as explained in "58. Support a Virtual Office with Collaboration on Your Network."

The children can swap ideas, sketches, figures, and even share applications when necessary for developing the project.

74 Turn Screen Savers into Brain Feeders

Don't think that screen savers are mindless bits of visual flotsam that take over when you've run out of both useful and useless things to do. Some are entirely educational—almost out of this world. Look at what screen savers can do in the search for extraterrestrial intelligence and for studying the physics of gravity. By storing the programs on your server, you can also put the screen savers on any of your PCs.

Make Your Network Part of the SETI Project

Your network can become an important part of the search for extraterrestrial intelligence. You don't need an advanced degree or gobs of money—only some unused time on your PCs.

The SETI (Search for Extra-Terrestrial Intelligence) project involves the rigorous mathematical analysis of veritable mountains of data. Scientists behind the venture didn't have banks of super computers sitting in a back room, so they took an innovative approach. Rather than perform all the analysis in the lab, their own computers divvy up the work and send it out to volunteers.

The volunteers run a special screen saver. When the computer is online and idle, the screen saver obtains data from the SETI@home server, analyzes it, and then returns the data. Here's how to become part of the project with Windows 95 or 98 PCs:

1. SETI@home asks people to download software from only their site at `setiathome.ssl.berkeley.edu`. Follow the links on the page, and save the software to an empty directory.

2. Highlight the file in Windows Explorer, and double-click it.

3. Click Next, then Yes, Next twice more, and finally Finish.

4. Set the preferences for how you want the program to run, such as whether the analysis should run continuously and whether the screen saver can connect to the Internet automatically. Click OK.

5. Click OK again to create a new account. Fill in the information.

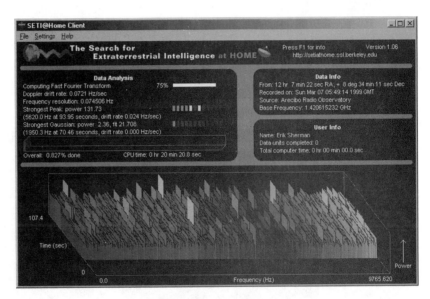

There are also versions of the software for many other types of computers. Be warned, though, the program uses lots of system resources, so if any of your PCs are older, less powerful machines, be sure to set the software to run only when the screen saver is either active or at the front of your screen. To change the settings, do the following:

1. Start the SETI@home software by clicking Start ➤ Programs ➤ SETI@home ➤ SETI@home.

2. Select Preferences from the Settings menu.

3. Configure the program, and then click OK.

Now your computer can chip in, if you will, on SETI data analysis.

Study Physics with the Gravitation Screen Saver

If space is on your mind, you might find yourself pulled to the physics of gravity. The Gravitation screen saver uses accurate mathematical equations to model how a number of heavenly bodies would interact. You can also change values of the parameters to affect the movement of the bodies.

If you would like to give this screen saver a try, do the following:

1. Download the program from members.tripod.com/~lpi/index.html, and save it to an empty directory. Use a program like Winzip or PKZIP to unpack the zip file.

2. Double-click Setup.exe in the same directory.

3. Click Next twice and you are ready to use the screen saver.

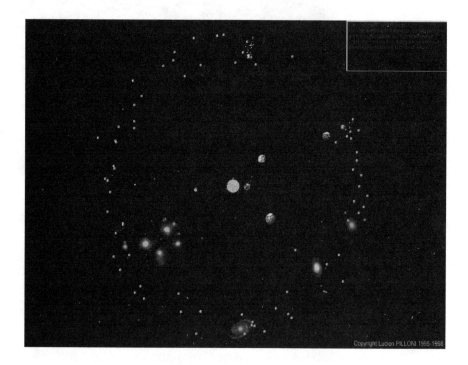

For information on how to configure the screen saver, see the screen saver Web site (members.tripod.com/~lpi/index.html). The author of Gravitation has other screen savers, too, though with a less educational bent.

Will this screen saver make you an Einstein? No, but it's a good conversation substitute for other weighty matters.

75 Turn Your Network into a Virtual Planetarium with SkyGlass

Children and adults alike can be taken with the stars. Typically, larger cities have planetariums, but with a computer network, it doesn't matter where you live.

 SkyGlass is a shareware program that lets you view the stars, click on individual points, and learn about them. You can install the program to individual PCs, or you can actually run it over your network:

1. Install the program with the user interface on the CD accompanying this book, or install manually by double-clicking the file Setup.exe in the directory \Network as Learning Lab\SkyGlass\ on the CD.

2. From any PC on your network, double-click the file SkyGlass.exe.

You can move about the night skies at your leisure, even choosing particular locations by longitude and latitude or specific times and dates. To find information on any planet, star, or constellation, click on it. You get an information box.

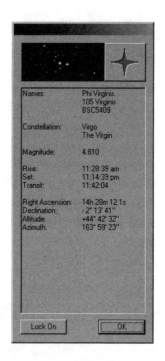

76 Learn about the Weather

As the old saying puts it, everyone talks about the weather, but no one does anything about it. Now you can follow the weather as closely as you want on your network with resources running from Web sites to software packages.

Use Your Network to Reach Weather Web Sites

For those who wish to learn about the weather, as well as for the true climate junkies, the Web is a marvelous place. AccuWeather (www.accuweather.com) provides many types of weather forecasts for locations around the world, in either metric or U.S. measurements. Here's some of the information you can get:

- ◆ See a five-day or six- to ten-day forecast for specific zip codes.
- ◆ View radar images of your area.
- ◆ Track hurricanes and tropical storms.
- ◆ Get weather maps for regions around the world, including Antarctica!
- ◆ Check your weather knowledge with a trivia page.
- ◆ Obtain a pilot's forecast if you fly your own plane.

Although you might think one weather source online would be enough, also look at the Weather Channel's Web site. Some of the services are the same, such as local weather and pilot forecasts, but many are different:

- ◆ Get three-day forecasts for many specific cities around the world.
- ◆ Check air quality and pollen reports for many metropolitan areas.
- ◆ See 3-D weather animations in Windows Media Player.

Aside from the articles on weather that both sites carry, grade school students can build projects with the data they collect over time.

Use Weather Software

If you want to take a more intimate look at the weather, programs such as Weather1 can keep you so up-to-date that you could become a bore at cocktail parties. An evaluation copy of the product is on the CD accompanying this book.

Weather1 pulls together information from various sites on the Internet, including

- ◆ Current weather conditions
- ◆ Forecasts
- ◆ Warnings and advisories
- ◆ Radar images
- ◆ Weather cams

Here's how to start the program:

1. Install the program with the user interface on the CD accompanying this book, or install manually by double-clicking the file Weather1.exe in the directory \Network as Learning Lab\Weather1\ on the CD.

2. Click Next.

3. Read the information on the product, and then click Next.

4. Click Browse to pick a location on your network server, and then click Next.

5. Select Yes to have backup copies of files, and then click Next three times. Click Finish.

6. Start the program by clicking Start ➢ Programs ➢ Weather1 ➢ Weather1.

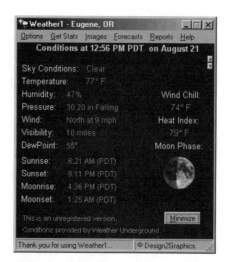

There are so many types of reports, images, forecasts, and other arcana that you could learn about just by going through the menus and looking up some of the possibilities.

77 Create a Network Reading Center

Unlike television, computers are—at least for now—intrinsically tied into the act of reading. What you might not know, though, is that your network can become a true reading center, housing plenty of outstanding reading material, much of it free, without taking up an inch of shelf space.

Then while you are stocking up on all manners of literature, history, and biography, you can bring them along on a hand-held computer or even use some clever software that can help you read faster.

Stock Your Network Bookshelf

The amount of material available for the asking on the Internet is astounding:

◆ The Electronic Library (`www.books.com/scripts/lib.exe`) is a free service offered by an online bookseller, Books.com. It provides text-file versions of titles that literally range from *Pinocchio* in the original Italian to translations of Marcus Aurelius in the nonoriginal English. Read Sir Richard Burton's translation of the *Arabian Nights,* or enjoy the screenplay of *Monty Python and the Holy Grail.*

◆ Project Gutenberg (`www.promo.net/pg/`) is an organization dedicated to providing free versions of titles that are in the public domain. According to Project Gutenberg, these fall into light literature, heavy literature, and even reference materials, such as *Roget's Thesaurus,* almanacs, dictionaries, and encyclopedias.

◆ The On-Line Books Page (`www.cs.cmu.edu/books.html`) is another directory of books available online. Because it is maintained by academics, there are not only works of literature and philosophy but also psychology, religion, science, various engineering disciplines, social sciences, and even military science to prepare for the odd battle. Expect to find scholarly titles here.

Bring Books with You

Once you have established your network book collection, you can download those files and bring them along. If you have a Windows CE device, you should be able to download either text or HTML books from your server.

Unfortunately, Palm organizers don't directly support either text files or HTML, but they support special document formats instead. MemoWare (www.memoware.com) has many downloadable books in document formats as well as links to a number of sites that have document readers. A particularly interesting one is iSilo (www.isilo.com). The company has both freeware and shareware readers as well as converters to change text and HTML files into its own format. So you can create your own versions of anything you want on your literature server.

Learn to Read Faster

With all the free books, you may feel overwhelmed. Keep your head. AceReader can help you learn to read faster. It does this in a number of ways:

◆ AceReader can read single words at a time from a text file and then flash them onto the center of the screen. By eliminating the time it takes to move your eye over a page, you spend less time reading.

◆ The program can also train your eye to move faster over a page by flashing several words at a time from one side of the screen to the other. Learning the technique of taking in groups of words will speed regular reading.

◆ There are options to increase the speed of either reading technique. Over time, you can force yourself to move faster through material.

◆ You can use tests that give you a preselected story and then time how quickly you move through the material. Several questions follow to give you a feeling for how well you absorbed the story.

To start training your eyes, install the software with the following steps:

1. Install the program with the user interface on the CD accompanying this book, or install manually by double-clicking the file acerd.exe in the directory \Network as Learning Lab\AceReader\ on the CD.

2. Click Next, then Yes, and Next twice more.

3. Decide whether you want a desktop shortcut for the program and whether you want to run it now.

4. Click Finish.

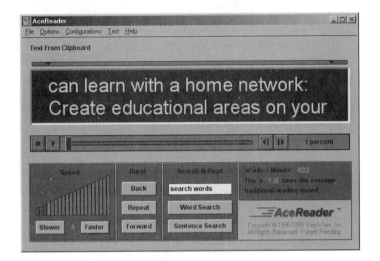

Although AceReader is designed to work with text files, you can select text in a word-processing or HTML document, copy it to the Clipboard, and then select Load Clipboard from the File menu.

Get Kids Reading

Roxie's Reading Fish is a program aimed at a younger audience. It uses a variation of the card game Go Fish, where players ask for cards with particular words on them.

Here are the steps to install an evaluation version of Roxie's Reading Fish:

1. Install the program with the user interface on the CD accompanying this book, or install manually by double-clicking the file rf.exe in the directory \Network as Learning Lab\Roxie's Reading Fish\ on the CD.

2. You should now see the file rf.exe. Double-click it.

3. Click Next twice, and then click Finish to install the program.

Make sure that your children use the program on a networked PC with a sound card and speakers, because the cat talks. To play the game, click Start ➤ Programs ➤ Roxie's Reading Fish ➤ Roxie's Reading Fish.

78 Learn Music on Your Network

You may have already created an MP3 server on your network, but now its time to become involved with music in a different way:

◆ Learn music theory.

◆ Write your own scores or songs.

◆ Experiment with modern and even otherworldly sounds.

There are many tutorials on music available on the Internet, to say nothing of software available to sharpen your skills and even compose music. In time, you might even make your own MP3 titles to add to your collection.

Learn Music Theory with Musical Tutorial

Musical Tutorial can't teach you everything about music theory, but it will help with learning the keyboard and how to better read music. It has a bias to the piano, but this is understandable, as it is traditionally the instrument of choice for learning music.

All you need to run Musical Tutorial on one of your networked PCs is either Windows 95 or 98 and a sound card with speakers. Installation is easy:

1. Install the program with the user interface on the CD accompanying this book, or install manually by double-clicking the file Setup.exe in the directory \Network as Learning Lab\Music Tutorial\ on the CD.

2. Click Next first and then the icon to install the program.

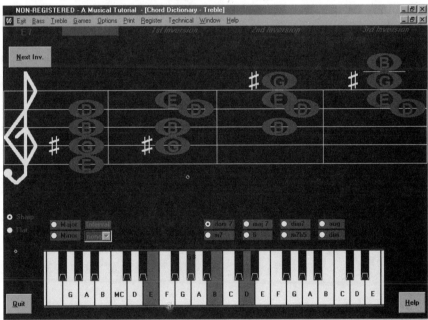

When installed, you can choose to drill on sight-reading, review chords, and work on scales.

Another program, The Music Box, focuses completely on ear training, or the ability to associate the music you hear with notes on a page. To install the program, do the following:

1. Install the program with the user interface on the CD accompanying this book, or install manually by double-clicking the file Setup.exe in the directory \Network as Learning Lab\Music Box\ on the CD.

2. To run the program from any PC on your network, use that computer's Windows Explorer to go to the Music Box directory, and then double-click the file Musbox32.exe.

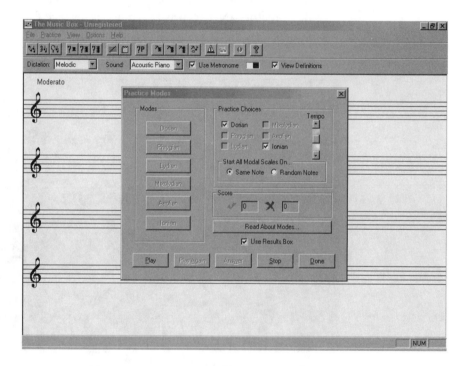

You can practice sight singing, interval training, pitch recognition, and other features that will improve your musical knowledge.

Write Your Own Scores or Songs

After working on the theory, practice with some composing. NoteWorthy Composer gives you the tools to create your magnum opus.

To start composing, first you need to install the program:

1. Install the program with the user interface on the CD accompanying this book, or install manually by double-clicking the file Setup.exe in the directory \Network as Learning Lab\Noteworthy Composer\ on the CD.

2. Click Next twice.

3. Select No, I Want to Evaluate the Program, and click Next twice.

4. Click Browse to choose a network directory, and then click Next twice.

5. Click Finish.

To start the program, click Start ➤ Programs ➤ NoteWorthy Composer, and then click I Accept to agree to the evaluation conditions.

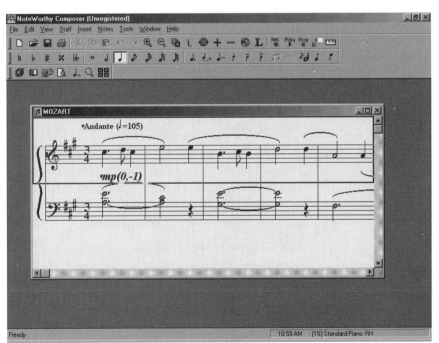

You can write new scores using the included templates or open some of the samples and turn yourself into a Beethoven.

79 Get Experience in the High-Paying Networking Field

In case you didn't know, your network gives anyone in your home a prime opportunity to learn skills that pay very well. Experienced network administrators and programmers are scarce and can command impressive salaries.

Your network offers a great learning tool:

◆ Add a Windows 2000 server and you can learn one of the hottest network operating systems around. Check out *Mastering Windows 2000 Professional,* by Mark Minasi and Todd Phillips (Sybex, 2000), for more information.

◆ Install a Linux server and get experience with networking under a Unix-like NOS. A good book on the subject is *Mastering Linux Premium Edition,* by Arman Danesh (Sybex, 1999), which includes a copy of Linux.

◆ Practice for some of the professional networking certifications a number of vendors offer. For example, check out *CCNA: Cisco Certified Network Associate Study Guide,* by Todd Lammle and Don Porter, with James Chellis (Sybex, 1998) and *Network+ Test Success,* by David Groth and Matthew M. Perkins (Sybex, 1999).

◆ Let your children gain practice at maintaining a network. This will give them marketable abilities that pay far better at an after-school job and in the summer than scooping ice cream.

The best advantage is that you don't have to travel to a classroom or training facility to have access to a network for practice.

80 Adult Education on Your Network

Learning away from a traditional campus has come a long way. With the Web and your network, you have an expansive number of choices in furthering your education:

- ◆ An increasing number of institutions of higher learning offer *distance learning* courses that provide college credit. Some—including name schools like Duke—offer accredited degrees with little or no presence on campus.

- ◆ A number of companies offer commercially priced training in various areas.

- ◆ You can find tutorials, not offered through a school or institution, on many topics, from bookbinding old paperbacks (`http://www.cs.uiowa.edu/~jones/book/`) to an introduction to celestial navigation (`peck.ipph.purdue.edu/al/space.html`). These are often free.

A high-speed Internet connection for your network will make the process fast-paced, at least in the delivery of information. If you see a course you like, consider saving it to the education directory on your file server. The Web is expansive and ephemeral, and what is available one day may be gone the next.

Play Multiplayer Games on Your Network

In playing computer games, you can say "The more, the merrier" when you have a computer network in your home. Rather than facing some nameless conglomeration of programming code, you can challenge friends and family in many ways:

◆ Play traditional card games.

◆ Combine civilization building with shoot 'em up action.

◆ Host your role-playing sessions.

◆ Invite players from outside your home to join in.

There are free and inexpensive games on the Internet as well as some good shareware on the CD accompanying this book.

81 Set Up Your Network to Run Multiplayer Games

Depending on the game, you can use your network to play against other people in a number of ways:

◆ You can log onto a multiplayer game over the Internet.

◆ You can play network-enabled games directly on your network.

◆ You can run software to connect your network to game players on the Internet.

◆ You can let friends dial-up your network.

Your choices may differ, depending on the game, but your network will make computer games a lot more fun.

Log onto Multiplayer Games over the Internet

Those who thrive on gaming can look to the Internet as a source for competition. Many games that have the capacity for multiple players also support special servers that facilitate matches, no matter where the contestants actually live.

In many cases, the game vendors run the servers. At other times, a third party may run them. A server may handle only one game or the games of a single vendor, or it may provide support for a variety of games.

N O T E Many multiuser sessions require you to own a copy of the particular game running.

Because games go in and out of fashion so quickly, your best bet is to check major search engines:

1. Pick a search engine. Yahoo.com or About.com are particularly good choices, because they put links into categories.

2. Enter a Search term. You might try "game servers" or "multiplayer."

3. Also try searching for the name of the game you want to play.

Check some of the links you see until you find a server that seems responsive and that supports the game that has your interest.

Play Multiuser Games on Your Network

Most multiuser games support play on a peer-to-peer network, so you are well set. Buy a copy of the game for each person who will play. Install the game on the networked PCs, and then follow the vendor's instructions on playing over a network.

N O T E You may need to run a particular network protocol for a game. You would think TCP/IP would be most common with the Internet, but many game companies like Novell's IPX protocol because it is faster than TCP/IP. If you see an unintelligible error, the game may be looking for IPX. Try adding IPX to your network, according to the steps in "19. Let Computers Talk with a Network Protocol."

Run Software to Connect Your Network to Game Players on the Internet

This is an intriguing approach. Besides playing with people on your own network, you can add others over the Internet, which means friends, no matter where their location, can join in.

In general, this is how to host games on the Internet:

1. Establish a high-speed connection from your network to the Internet.

2. Locate software that lets you host an Internet multiuser session for a particular game.

3. Install the multiuser software.

4. Install copies of the game on the networked PCs you plan to use.

5. Inform the remote players of the IP address they need to use. Check your proxy server or Internet sharing software to see what that would be.

You may need to do some digging on search engines to see whether there is multiuser hosting software for the specific game that interests you. For example, the game Starcraft from Blizzard Entertainment is popular. Although Blizzard has a server for multiplayer games called Battle.net, you can download free server software called *FSGS*, or Free Standard Game Server (www.fsgs.com). The site has directions on how to set up the software, and there are versions for a variety of operating systems, including Windows 95 and 98.

The game Warpath 97 from Synthetic Reality (see "82. Colonize Planets and Have Interstellar Battles with Warpath 97") has a free multiuser program to accept players from the Internet.

1. Copy the file mix.exe from the \Play Games on Network\Mix directory on the CD accompanying this book to a directory on the PC with the network Internet connection.

2. Double-click the file. There is no installation routine.

3. Enter a TCP/IP port number, such as 24000.

4. Click Accept Calls.

If you want to make your server available to the general public, select "Register as a Public Server." The software then registers with Synthetic Reality's directory of servers.

Let Friends Dial Up Your Network

You can let friends dial-up your network. By running whatever protocol is required by the game, they should be able to play with you. To set up a dial-up connection, see "22. Remotely Access Your Home Network with a Windows 98 Dial-Up Server."

82 Colonize Planets and Have Interstellar Battles with Warpath 97

You can mine ore, trade for money, invest in colonies, and shoot the other guy first. It's a fairly straight description of Warpath 97, which is a shareware game. Although you can play on your own, it is more fun to compete with others.

N O T E You need to run IPX, the NetWare protocol, to run Warpath 97 in Multiuser mode on your network. You don't need to run NetWare, however. See "19. Let Computers Talk with a Network Protocol."

First you have to install the game:

1. Install the program with the user interface on the CD accompanying this book, or install manually by double-clicking the file Warpath97.exe in the directory \Play Games on Network\Warpath 97 on the CD.

2. Click OK, Unzip, and then OK.

3. Click Close to close the self-extractor.

4. To start the game, go to the directory C:\warpath97. Double-click warpath97.exe.

5. Click New Game.

6. Select Multiplayer Game.

7. Choose IPX LAN from the pick list under "Select Preferred Network from this List."

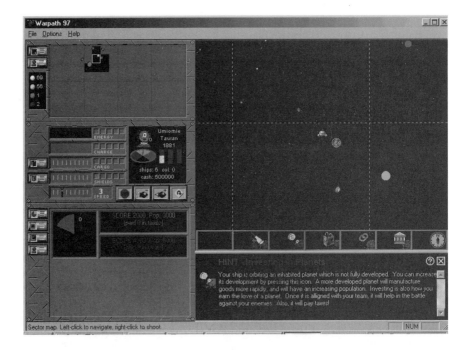

You can now compete with others to colonize planets and invest in their future, as you blow up anyone who gets in your way.

83 Play a Traditional Card Game Such As Hearts

You can host a card game on your network without any work at all. Windows 95 and 98 come with a version of Hearts that is multiuser:

1. Click Start ➤ Programs ➤ Accessories ➤ Games ➤ Hearts.

2. Type your name into the space on the dialog box.

3. One player should select "I Want to be Dealer."

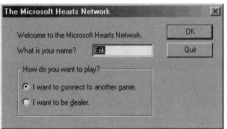

4. Click OK.

5. If you choose "I Want to Connect to Another Game, the program prompts you for the network name of the computer the dealer is using. Type it in, and click OK.

Up to four people on your network can play at a time.

84 Quake Your Network

If you like QuakeWorld from id Software, you will enjoy running the game on your network. To do so, you need a server. Local QuakeWorld is a freeware server that runs on Windows 95, 98, or NT 4.

Here's how to get the server running:

1. Download a copy of the program `qwlocl.zip` from www.zdnet.com to the directory from which you will run the program.

2. Unarchive the program with a program such as Winzip or PKZIP.

3. After it has extracted itself, double-click `qwlocal.exe`.

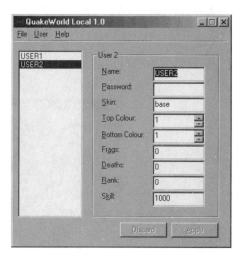

4. To add a user, select Add from the User menu. Fill out the particulars for all the users of the game, and then minimize the dialog box.

You are now ready to play with other people or friends on your network.

INDEX

Note to the Reader: Throughout this index **boldfaced** page numbers indicate primary discussions of a topic. *Italicized* page numbers indicate illustrations.

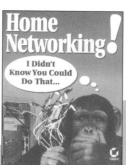

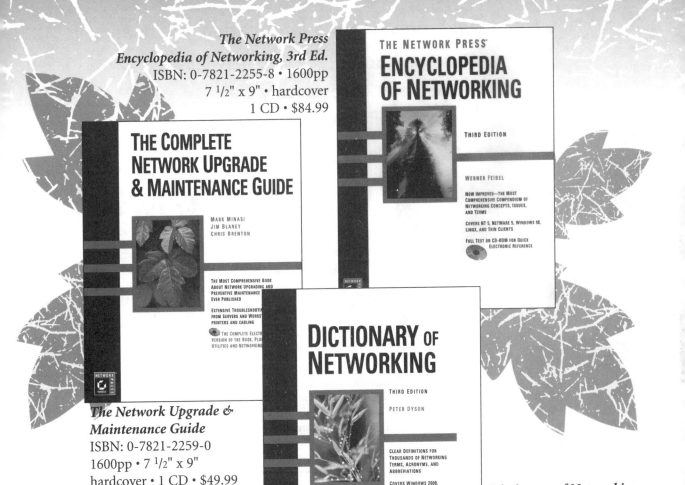
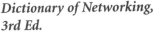

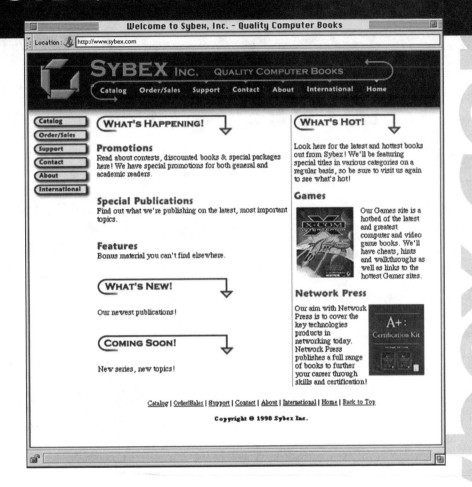

About the CD

You can find two types of content on the CD sitting at the back of this book. One type is software. From programs that keep you organized to business software and even entertainment and games, you can undoubtedly find something to your interest. Some of it is shareware, and other programs are absolutely free. In addition to software, you will also find special offers from some of the vendors in this book that can save you a lot of money. Here's what you can look forward to:

Antivirus Software

VirusNet LAN

VirusNet PC

Network Utilities

MacDrive98

PC MACLAN for Windows 95/98

Personal MACLAN for Windows 3.1

SMARTmonitor

SAPS Modem Sharing Software

SyShield

MP3 Server Software

MP3 Database

MusicMatch Jukebox

RealPlayer G2

RealJukebox

Connectivity Software

Harmony

Webetc Proxy Server